Take Better Pictures

An amateur photographer book

Take Better Pictures
An amateur photographer book

Martin Hodder

This edition produced exclusively for
WHSMITH

Contents

This edition published exclusively for WH Smith

Published by
The Hamlyn Publishing Group Limited
London · New York · Sydney · Toronto
Astronaut House, Feltham, Middlesex, England.
Copyright © The Hamlyn Publishing Group Limited 1981

ISBN 0 600 35594 2
Printed in England

The rudiments of photography

Light is the raw material of photography, as necessary for the photographic image as it is for life itself. The word photography actually means 'drawing with light', and there was a time when the artist did exactly that: he used a pencil to trace over an image formed in a *camera obscura* (dark chamber) in much the same way as it is formed in a modern camera. Nowadays the process relies on chemistry rather than on a man with a pencil.

Any light can be harnessed for the creation of photographic images: sunlight is the most commonly used, but moonlight, domestic lamps, photofloods, flash, street lamps and neon street signs, candles, even the distant stars can all be used for photography given suitable equipment— which need not be complicated or expensive—and a certain amount of knowhow.

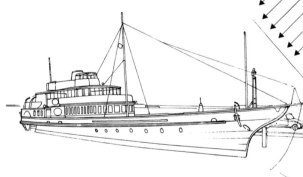

The **camera** is the instrument used to collect the light reflected (or produced) by the chosen subject. The camera body could do this alone by means of a tiny 'pinhole' opening in the front, but unfortunately this simple method is too slow to be practicable. The trouble is that if the pinhole is enlarged to speed the process up, the sharp image degenerates into an indecipherable blur of light and shade. To control the light entering the camera, and bring it into focus even when the opening is large, a lens is fitted. Modern lenses comprise a number of glass elements designed to bend (refract) light, so that it forms a precise image rapidly and in a wide range of conditions.

The **subject** is anything you see that you wish to preserve in picture form: it may be a person, a place, a thing, an event, a pattern of light, or a combination of any of these. Your approach to it may be literal or interpretative. Provided it either reflects light from elsewhere (as in a sunlit landscape) or contains one or more sources of light in itself (as in a city street at night) it can be photographed. Examples of good photographic subjects—some of them obvious, others less so—are described in detail with demonstration photographs on pages 72-129, together with advice on how to tackle them.

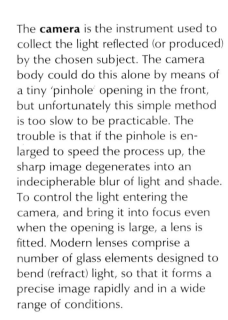

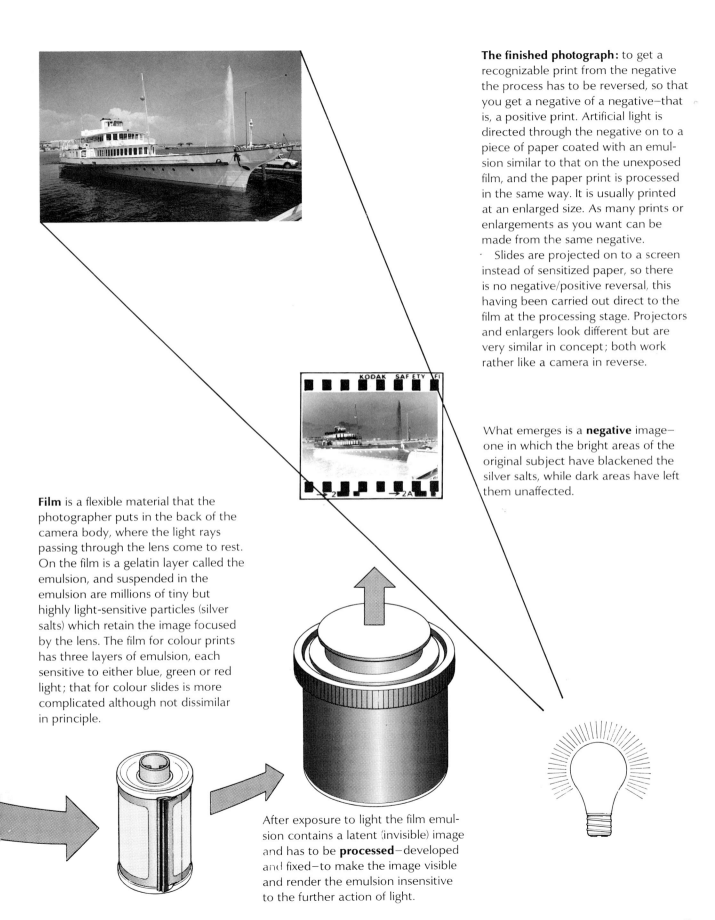

The finished photograph: to get a recognizable print from the negative the process has to be reversed, so that you get a negative of a negative—that is, a positive print. Artificial light is directed through the negative on to a piece of paper coated with an emulsion similar to that on the unexposed film, and the paper print is processed in the same way. It is usually printed at an enlarged size. As many prints or enlargements as you want can be made from the same negative.

Slides are projected on to a screen instead of sensitized paper, so there is no negative/positive reversal, this having been carried out direct to the film at the processing stage. Projectors and enlargers look different but are very similar in concept; both work rather like a camera in reverse.

What emerges is a **negative** image—one in which the bright areas of the original subject have blackened the silver salts, while dark areas have left them unaffected.

Film is a flexible material that the photographer puts in the back of the camera body, where the light rays passing through the lens come to rest. On the film is a gelatin layer called the emulsion, and suspended in the emulsion are millions of tiny but highly light-sensitive particles (silver salts) which retain the image focused by the lens. The film for colour prints has three layers of emulsion, each sensitive to either blue, green or red light; that for colour slides is more complicated although not dissimilar in principle.

After exposure to light the film emulsion contains a latent (invisible) image and has to be **processed**—developed and fixed—to make the image visible and render the emulsion insensitive to the further action of light.

13

Choosing a camera

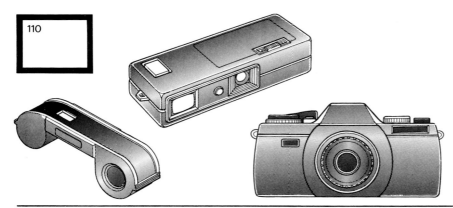

Pocket cameras that take 110 film are economical, small, and simple to load and use; they are suitable for the photographer who does not require very large prints: up to enprint size (as commonly supplied by processing houses) they give excellent results. Some offer the slightly more ambitious photographer a range of interesting features. The tiny single-lens reflexes taking 110 cartridges are marvels of miniaturization and can compete with any camera for versatility. Further information: page 16.

Although using a larger negative size than 110, the 126 cameras are mostly very simple and cheap. They are widely used, but are not suitable for really large prints—however, their shortcomings are hardly noticeable at normal print sizes. The Kodak 'Instamatic' and other 126 cameras are excellent for children and beginners who want to make photographs without being distracted by technical detail. They give square prints 9×9cm ($3\frac{1}{2} \times 3\frac{1}{2}$in) in size. Further information: pages 16-17.

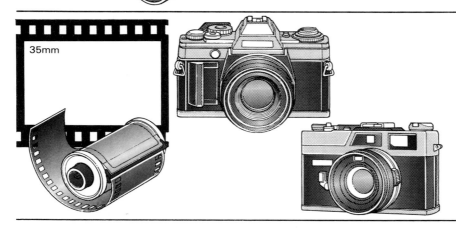

For the majority of real enthusiasts the 35mm film format represents the ideal balance of compactness, versatility and image quality. There are inexpensive compacts providing good quality for the least effort; there are fully automatic models for those who want good quality in any lighting conditions but still for little effort, and there are extra-ordinarily versatile reflex cameras which offer the photographer complete control over his work. Many types of film are available. Further information: pages 18-21.

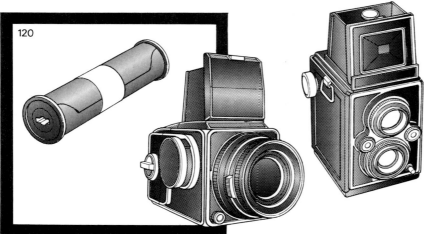

120 rollfilm is used in twin-lens reflexes and medium format single-lens reflexes, and produces square negatives which are 6×6cm ($2\frac{1}{4} \times 2\frac{1}{4}$in) in size—or occasionally 6×7cm ($2\frac{1}{4} \times 2\frac{3}{4}$in) when a rectangular format is preferred. Of all the cameras described here, these are the most expensive both to buy and to use, but there is no doubt that they give the highest quality results. Such cameras are less mobile than the 35mm types and are therefore more often used in controlled conditions than for action photography; however, the single-lens reflexes in particular are as adaptable as their 35mm counterparts, in some ways more so. Further information: pages 20-22.

Looking at the multitude of cameras on the market today can be a confusing experience. For one thing they come in so many shapes and sizes, yet they all operate according to the pattern described on the previous two pages: so the buyer will want to know what accounts for these differences. For another, rival manufacturers' claims regarding 'simplicity' often seem to be curiously at variance—for one it represents cheapness and lack of facilities, while for another it appears to represent the ultimate in microchip complexity.

If you have not already decided what you want, the following guidelines should help you to do so.

First choose a format rather than a camera. The larger the format the better the quality, although this is not very noticeable if only small prints are made. For most amateurs it comes down to a choice between 110 and 35mm, with 126 and 120 as possible alternatives.

Up to enprint size the 110 format gives excellent results. At greater enlargements the grain (the particle basis of the negative image) becomes increasingly obtrusive, so if you want large prints made go for 35mm. If you are sure that enprints are all you want, the 110 format has more to offer in terms of pocketability and simplicity of loading.

Medium and large-format cameras, taking 120 rollfilm, give superb results and are much used by professional studio photographers and dedicated amateurs. They are less mobile than the smaller formats and the photographer must expect to work harder for every picture taken; also, photography at this level is a considerably more expensive business.

Decide your budget before you start handling cameras in the showroom, otherwise you may easily find yourself being drawn into a price bracket where you do not really need to be. One of the consequences of the fierce competition prevalent in the photographic equipment market is that you tend to get what you pay for—but shop around, and do not be in a hurry to buy.

Consider what facilities you need: both 110 and 35mm (or 135) cameras are available with endless permutations of features—motor drives, zoom lenses, built-in flash, automatic exposure control and others. Some of these are not particularly useful for general photography, while others are. Their uses are described in more detail elsewhere in this book, so when considering a particular model, you can look its special features up and decide whether they will really be relevant to your own photographic ambitions.

This brings us back to the question of format. In general the photographers who want large prints, or transparencies projected to high magnifications, are also the ones most likely to be interested in versatile equipment and special features. Therefore there are more 35mm systems with elaborate lenses and accessories than any other type of camera. Conversely, photographers who are happy with a few sets of enprints at holiday time are less likely to be interested in learning to use complicated systems, so the trend is for 110 cameras to be basic or to offer only a limited range of additional features.

However, there are exceptions to suit photographers who do not fit comfortably into either trend. There are 110 systems which are miniature versions of sophisticated single-lens reflexes, e.g. the tiny Pentax auto 110 SLR system, or the Minolta 110 Zoom SLR. On the other hand simplicity of use and the higher quality offered by the 35mm film format are combined in a large and very popular group of cameras known as 'compacts', and for many people one of these represents the ideal compromise.

One other type should be mentioned: the instant picture camera. This is rather a special case, not directly comparable to the other types mentioned here, and is treated separately on pages 26-27.

The chart opposite summarizes the differences between camera types with their pros and cons. More detailed analyses of each type in turn are given on the following pages.

A photograph like that on the left could be taken with any camera, as the light is good and the subject not too close. Even the reeds in the foreground are far enough away to be in focus, especially if only a small print is to be made. For a picture like that on the right you need an adjustable camera—one which will focus on a subject as little as 50cm (15in) away and which has exposure controls to allow for the relatively dim light.

Pocket cameras — 110 and 126 film cartridges

The 110 pocket cameras have certain advantages over their larger and more expensive 35mm rivals, and one real disadvantage, which nevertheless will not concern everyone. The following are their advantages:

They are *pocketable*. The film cartridges are really small, and the camera and all its parts are correspondingly reduced in size. It will fit into a pocket or handbag, which means that it can be carried around at times when a bulkier camera might get left behind. For this reason you are unlikely to miss a picture because one day you decided not to take it with you.

They are *simple* in both design and use, at least at the basic end of the range. With a cartridge there is no threading of film on to a take-up spool—you simply load it into the camera and close the back, then wind on the film; sometimes you also have to set the film speed, although more often this is done automatically by means of notches in the cartridge.

The *choice* is enormous and ranges from the utterly simple to the extremely sophisticated, so that there is a model to suit almost every type of photography. The miniature single-lens reflexes at the top end of the market have enough features and refinements to rival some of the 35mm models described on pages 20-21, and

although it is inevitable that the more adjustments you have to make the less simple the operation becomes, every feature has been designed with ease of use in mind, and no one need worry that they will prove to be obstacles rather than aids to getting better pictures.

The *price* varies as the choice does. The cheapest models are very modest in price, whereas you can pay quite a lot for advanced ones, and at this stage it may be worthwhile reconsidering the 35mm compacts and single-lens reflexes.

The disadvantage common to all 110 cameras is that very big enlargements will never match the quality of those made to the same size from 35mm negatives, although with modern fine-grain films the results are better than they used to be. However,

even the cheapest have good quality lenses and will give satisfactory results at enprint size (i.e. about 12 × 9cm, slightly smaller than an ordinary postcard).

The word 'Instamatic' is a Kodak trade name and refers to the instant-loading capability of the cameras so designated and not, as some people believe, to any system of producing finished prints within moments of taking a picture.

Of more traditional appearance than the 110 pocket camera, the 126 was the first cartridge-loading system to go on sale and for a long time was extremely popular. Recently it has been losing ground to the 110 as the leader in the cartridge-loading field, largely because of the improved fine-grain films which make an enlargement from a 110 negative almost as

Left: 110 film gives rectangular prints slightly smaller than postcard size, the proportions of which are shown by the solid line. This line represents the normal image area of a 110 pocket camera. The inner (broken) line should be used for framing close-up shots; the reason for this is more fully explained in the caption to the picture on page 18.

Left: 110 pocket cameras can be obtained with a wide variety of additional features. The inexpensive Agfamatic 1008 (top right), the most basic in the Agfa range, has no special features – others in the range have motor winders, built-in flash and telephoto or macro lenses. The Sporti 440T (top left) has built-in flash and a telephoto lens. The Kodak Ektralite 400 (bottom right) has built-in flash and a steadying handle; while the Pentax Auto 110 SLR is a sophisticated system camera with many optional features which can all be purchased together as a complete set in its own carrying case.

Commercial processors usually supply prints 9 × 9cm (3½ × 3½in) square – i.e. somewhat smaller than shown on the left–from 126 film. Enlargements can be specifically ordered, although this costs more and it is probably worth reserving this treatment for your very best pictures.

Below: two cameras from the Kodak 'Instamatic' range. The 77X (right) is a very basic model, requiring no adjustments by the user except that flash cubes can be inserted in the socket on top. The 277X (left) can be used in a wider range of conditions – it is adjusted by means of a rotating ring on the lens marked with weather symbols, clearly visible in this picture, and there is a distance scale underneath for accurate focusing. This model also accepts flash cubes.

good as one from a 126 negative, even though the former is less than half as big.

The remarks about simplicity, and price made about 110 cameras apply equally to the 126 types.

The common categories of film– black and white print film, colour negative and colour reversal film–are available in both formats, but within these categories the choice is restricted to films of the following speeds (figures in brackets give numbers of exposures commonly available per film):

Film availability chart

	110	126
Colour negative film	80 ASA (12, 20) 100 ASA (12, 24) 400 ASA (12, 24)	80 ASA (12, 20) 100 ASA (12, 24)
Colour reversal film	64 ASA (20)	64 ASA (20) 100 ASA (20)
Black and white film	125 ASA (12)	125 ASA (12, 20)

35mm compacts and rangefinder cameras

The cameras generally known as compacts have elements in common with both the 110 and 126 cartridge-loading cameras described on the previous pages and with 35mm single-lens reflexes. They differ from the former in that they use the larger 35mm film size, and from the latter in that they have a direct-vision view-finding system and a fixed lens. Lens quality is generally excellent, and advanced models with built-in ex-posure meters and/or automatic exposure control produce results which can rival the best SLRs in quality, if not in versatility. If quality is more important than handiness and plain simplicity a 35mm compact will certainly be a better choice than either a 110 pocket camera or a 126 Instamatic.

The following is a summary of their important points:

In *size* compacts are smaller than single-lens reflexes and about the same as the Instamatics; although they are larger than 110 pocket cameras they are still often small enough to be truly pocketable.

The *lens quality* naturally varies to a certain extent with price, but on average is excellent. There is an improvement in image definition noticeable even at enprint size, but when photographs are enlarged to say 20·3 × 25·4cm (8 × 10in) the difference is far more marked. If you want prints at this size you should avoid the small formats altogether and go for 35mm or larger.

Compacts are reasonable in *price*, although sophisticated models can still cost a fair amount of money. A medium-price compact with built-in exposure meter compares very favour-ably with an equivalent single-lens reflex because of the relative simplicity of assembling a camera with one fixed lens and direct-vision viewfinder.

They are also *quiet* in operation compared to SLRs because the shutter release mechanism is less complicated.

Rangefinder cameras
A rangefinder is an optical device used to establish the distance from camera to subject so that the lens

can be accurately focused. Any modern camera with a direct-vision viewfinder and focusing lens will almost certainly have a built-in rangefinder, but there are many older models still in use which do not, and independent rangefinders can be purchased for use with these.

Strictly speaking, to lump 'range-finder cameras' together as a special category is to create artificial distinc-tions and resemblances, but in photo-graphic circles the term usually refers to 35mm cameras in which the range-finder image is adjusted by the move-ment of the focusing ring itself; this is

Above: the viewfinder of a 35mm com-pact camera typically shows more than the actual image area, the exact limits of which are indicated by the white 'bright line' frame. The secondary lines inside the main frame are for use in composing close-up pictures: since the viewfinder window is somewhat offset from the lens-to-subject axis, at close range it shows a slightly different image from that which will actually be recorded on film. This is called 'parallax'; the inner lines are 'parallax correction marks'. The top picture shows use of the outer (main) frame; the lower one demonstrates how the parallax correction marks are used for correct framing of close-up subjects.

Top left: an automatic compact which can be operated manually if the user prefers, the Ricoh 500 ME has a coupled rangefinder.

Top right: The Olympus Pen EE-3, an automatic with a fixed-focus lens, and which gives vertical format images covering only half of the normal negative area, so that you get double the number of exposures per roll of film.

Bottom left: the Regula picca c, which has a built-in exposure meter. There is an accurate distance scale and adjustable lens apertures and shutter speeds.

Bottom right: the Minolta Hi-Matic G2, a versatile little automatic camera with focusing by zone symbols or a distance scale, whichever the user finds easier.

otherwise known as the *coupled rangefinder* system. In some older cameras the rangefinder has a separate viewing window, so that once the photographer had focused the lens on his subject he had to transfer his eye back to the viewfinder in order to frame the shot. Nowadays the rangefinder is incorporated in the viewfinder window.

Few photographers are interested in using interchangeable lenses except with reflex viewing, but there are some exceptions. They prefer the rangefinder system on account of its quieter operation and the overall clarity of the direct-vision viewfinder, but are not prepared to dispense with the interchangeable lens facility. There are a few system rangefinder cameras on the market to cater for their needs, notably very expensive models such as the Minolta CLE and, at the other end of the scale, cheap models such as the Russian-made Kiev 4 and Fed 4L series.

Any camera with a fixed-focus lens is set to give a picture that is sharp from perhaps 2m (6ft) in front of the camera to infinity. The picture on the right shows quite clearly that this is possible, although the light needs to be reasonably good.

Single-lens reflexes

The feature which sets single-lens reflex cameras apart from the other types is the mirror by which the image in the lens is diverted into the viewfinder—thus the photographer is actually looking through the lens at *exactly* the same image as will be formed on the film. When the shutter release is pressed the mirror swings out of the way, then the shutter opens and closes to make the exposure, and finally in most models the mirror swings back to its original position, restoring the momentarily blacked-out image to the viewfinder.

There are definite advantages to this system. The most obvious is that the image in the viewfinder is the same as that which will fall on the film at the moment of exposure, so the photographer is less likely to make disappointing 'mistakes' in composition.

The reflex viewing system makes possible another great advantage: the standard lens can be removed and another put in its place. Before the development of reflex cameras it was not really practical to use lenses outside a relatively restricted range of focal lengths—the viewfinder and the lens did not 'see' the same image, and so the photographer could not be

The viewfinder of a typical SLR: the set shutter speed (left) and aperture (top) are displayed, while the needle coupled with the exposure meter indicates whether the settings are correct for the conditions.

When the shutter of a 35mm SLR is released, (1) the lens diaphragm closes down to the preset stop; (2) the mirror swings up, blocking the light path to the viewfinder; (3) the shutter opens and closes, making the exposure; (4) the mirror returns to its original position, and (5) the diaphragm reopens.

sure of what he was getting on the film. But once he found himself looking down the lens that was actually being used to make the picture, the possibilities began to open up. Extreme telephoto lenses could be used to magnify distant objects in much the same way as a pair of binoculars (or more accurately, a telescope); conversely, extreme wide-angle and fisheye lenses could be fitted, giving a kind of image that was new to photography. These lenses are further described on pages 138–143.

Most single-lens reflex cameras are designed for either 35mm film or the larger-format 6×6cm ($2\frac{1}{4} \times 2\frac{1}{4}$in) rollfilm. Those designed for the latter format are generally so expensive as to be of interest more to the professional and really dedicated amateur than to the beginner or average enthusiast—much of the fashion photography appearing in magazines such as *Vogue*, for example, is likely to have been taken with cameras such as the Hasselblad illustrated opposite.

The 35mm SLR is a different story. Cheap but adequate models are available at around the same price as some of the compacts or 110 pocket cameras. Lens quality is generally good and the 35mm negative (or transparency) is large enough to give high quality prints when enlarged (or

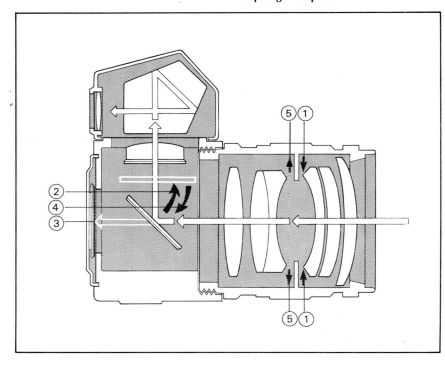

projected) to sizes acceptable for most purposes. Yet the body is small enough to be easily manageable—if not actually pocketable—and for people who need to take good quality pictures in awkward situations this is almost certainly the best choice. The majority of Press photographers use 35mm SLRs.

One more type of single-lens reflex camera must be mentioned: the 110 cartridge-loading SLR. Cameras of this type combine all the basic features of the 35mm models with the 110 film format. This may be a good choice of camera where the 35mm models are too bulky.

There is a wide-ranging armoury of accessories available to the SLR user. Some of these are described on pages 148-149, although many of them will be of interest only to the experienced photographer. However it is worth bearing in mind when choosing a camera that you are never likely to have to discard your 35mm SLR because you do not find it versatile enough.

There are various reasons for the huge differences in price between basic and complex SLRs. The quality of the lens fitted as standard varies

from model to model, as does the robustness of the body itself and the range of features built into it. Even the simplest types have focusing, aperture and shutter speed control, usually a depth of field preview facility, a means of connecting a flash unit, delayed action shutter release and some means of double exposure prevention. You pay more for varying degrees of automation (see pages 24-25) and for outright quality and reliability of lens and body.

Quick framing and shooting are possible in single-lens reflex photography, which makes it the ideal medium for capturing moments of street life such as this. A moderate telephoto lens helps to get the subject big and clear in the view-finder, and need not be an expensive addition to your range of equipment (one of 135mm focal length was fitted in this case).

Some examples of SLR equipment. Left the Ricoh KR-10, an aperture priority automatic SLR with full manual over-ride, but which costs only a little more than some basic SLRs. Right: the Canon A-1, a space-age product, is more expensive but offers five automatic exposure modes and a variety of electronic features too numerous to list. Below left: the Hasselblad; for ultra-high quality results combined with the benefits of reflex viewing this type of camera is hard to beat, but the cost is high. Below right: a range of lenses made by Soligor to fit 35mm SLRs. Such lenses can be added to the basic outfit as and when your budget permits.

Twin lens reflexes

The twin-lens reflex (TLR) was introduced before the single-lens reflex and its design is simple in principle: in effect it consists of two box cameras placed one on top of the other, each with an identical lens. The upper box contains a mirror and a focusing screen and is used for viewing; the lower box contains the film and is used for taking the picture. The upper lens focuses the image via the mirror on to the screen, which is situated above and at right-angles to the film plane; the image focused by the lower lens on to the film is identical, or nearly so (at close range parallax introduces a discrepancy which the photographer has to allow for). The focusing of the two lenses is mechanically linked, which is what differentiates the TLR from viewfinder cameras.

Provided that the viewing lens has the same focal length as the taking lens, and is good enough to allow accurate framing and focusing, it need not be of the same high quality. The twin-lens design is therefore not as wasteful of precision optics as may appear at first sight.

The TLR is a camera for the enthusiast. It is not as simple in use as the 35mm SLR. For one thing the viewing image is reversed left to right, which many amateurs find disconcerting, especially when trying to follow a moving subject. Also, in its standard form the camera is held at chest or waist level because the viewing image is in a horizontal plane—with the corollary that it can also be held upside-down above the head, giving the photographer an immense height advantage in certain circumstances (e.g. when crowds are lining the street to watch the passage of some celebrity or other). The ground glass viewing screen presents a flat two-dimensional image to the photographer instead of the direct-vision image found in basic cameras, a system which has passionate devotees but which does not suit everyone.

On the credit side, most TLRs utilize 120 rollfilm to give negatives or slides measuring 6 × 6cm

$(2\frac{1}{4} \times 2\frac{1}{4}in)$, which is considerably larger than the 35mm image area. Sections of the negative can be enlarged to enormous sizes without being spoiled by grain. The mechanics of TLRs are quite simple. There is no hinged mirror as there is in SLRs, and there is no built-in exposure meter, so there is much less to go wrong. This is

Right: the upper lens of a twin-lens reflex such as this Rolleiflex is for viewing; the lower lens is for making the actual exposure. Since the optical systems are separate there is no image black-out at the moment of exposure.

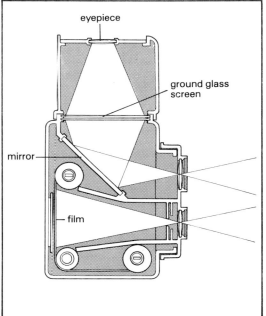

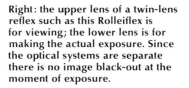

Left: diagram showing the light path through the two lenses of a twin-lens reflex camera. The image seen in the viewfinder appears reversed left to right (as shown below), and some practice may be needed before you get used to this, especially when trying to pan a moving subject. The shutter is built into the lower lens and is quiet and vibration-free in use. The mechanics of this type of camera are quite simple, so they can reasonably be expected to last for a long time. The 6 × 6cm $(2\frac{1}{4} \times 2\frac{1}{4}in)$ square format is large enough to yield superb pictures whatever type of film is used.

one of the reasons why examples of some early models, such as the original Rolleiflex, are still in active service today.

Most TLRs are not made with interchangeable lens systems, because both lenses have to be changed together, pushing up the cost. However the Mamiya range is an exception, having a range of lenses of different focal lengths manufactured for it.

Other types of camera

The cameras described on the foregoing pages are the kinds commonly found on sale for amateur use today. But since photography began there have been hundreds of variations on the basic box-with-lens combination at varying levels of complexity and specialization, and a visit to a second-hand shop or to one which specializes in catering for the professional will certainly bring to light some wonderful pieces of equipment that are unmistakably cameras, but which bear only a passing resemblance to the ones described here. This book is primarily intended for the owners—actual or potential—of modern mass-produced cameras, but the principles of photography are the same now as they always were and most of the information given on exposure, lighting, approach to subject and so on applies equally to any camera.

Left: a Kodak Regent. This early rollfilm camera was designed to take eight exposures on 620 film, giving large rectangular negatives. The lens is an f/4.5 Zeiss Tessar and shutter speeds range from 1 second to 1/400 second. It also has a coupled rangefinder.

A Kodak Retinette, dating from the days before automation became common. There is a window for a built-in exposure meter, although this particular model does not have one. It takes 35mm film and has a 40mm lens.

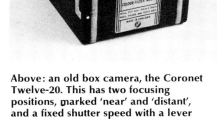

A Zeiss Ikon Ikonta, still capable of yielding excellent results. Shutter speed range is 1/25-1/75 second and the lens aperture is variable between f/4.5 and f/16. It takes film size 127, which gives negatives 4 × 3cm (1½ × 1⅛ in) or in other formats, all 4 centimetres wide. This film is relatively uncommon and is not described elsewhere in this book.

Above: an old box camera, the Coronet Twelve-20. This has two focusing positions, marked 'near' and 'distant', and a fixed shutter speed with a lever for time exposure. It takes 120 rollfilm.

The Leica III. Made by the company which was responsible for introducing the 35mm format, the Leicas are exceptionally rugged and reliable. The one illustrated is a rangefinder model with interchangeable lenses.

Automation — cameras that do it all

As with every other facet of camera design, the nature and degree of automation in 'automatic' cameras varies from range to range and from model to model. It is sometimes necessary to remind oneself that the purpose of automation is to make things easier rather than more complicated, and that however futuristic their descriptions or circuit diagrams may be, these cameras have removed a lot of technical drudgery and brought advanced camera technique within the reach of the outright beginner.

The most important of the camera functions which may be automated is exposure. It is relatively easy to understand what automatic exposure does, but not how it works.

If you are going to get satisfactory photos your film has to be correctly exposed, no matter what equipment you are using — this is a fundamental principle of photography. Correct exposure is explained elsewhere in this book (see pages 36-37); but using a camera with automatic exposure control *saves you the trouble of learning about correct exposure*. That, in ordinary language, is what automatic exposure is for.

To understand more about the subject you will need to have some idea of the relationship between shutter speed and lens aperture (pages 32-37) and of what built-in exposure meters do (pages 144-145).

In fully automatic (or fully programmed) systems the built-in exposure meter is connected directly to the camera controls: the photographer presses the shutter release and an electronic 'brain' in the camera sets the lens aperture and shutter speed. There may or may not be a read-out in the viewfinder to tell you what the settings are; there is usually some kind of warning if the light is too dim.

Semi-automatics demand a little more from the photographer — but not much, and they do extend his creative control. There are two systems, known as *aperture priority* and *shutter priority*. In the former the

Automatic exposure control averages out highlight and shadow areas, so that if the highlights are very bright the rest of the picture will be dense. The system automatically compensates for filters, such as the starburst used here.

Shutter priority automatic exposure systems enable the photographer to select a shutter speed that will stop movement; the camera selects the aperture to match.

photographer has to choose the lens aperture and the camera will compute and set the necessary shutter speed; in the latter these roles are reversed, the photographer choosing the shutter speed and the camera automatically setting the correct lens aperture. If you do not particularly want to worry about the effects of varying these settings, you may consider the semi-automatic systems an unnecessary refinement and, pocket permitting, you would probably do better to buy a fully automatic camera. If, on the other hand, you wish to explore the creative possibilities of photography, you will need one of the semi-automatics, or better still, one of the very sophisticated models which allows you to choose between aperture priority and shutter priority. Failing these (for example if money is a problem) you will want a camera with a built-in light meter and manual controls — i.e. one that is not automatic at all.

Automatic focusing is a system whereby the camera lens is automatically focused on the subject when the shutter release is pressed.

Above: two automatic cameras. The Ricoh A-2 is a 35mm compact with fully automatic exposure control. The Minolta XG-M is a single-lens reflex with aperture priority exposure control, including over and under compensation facility, and which continues to display the 'suggested' shutter speed together with the set speed even when the camera is being used in its manual mode.

Left: this sequence demonstrates the use of automatic focusing. If the subject is in the centre of the frame (top) the camera will focus correctly; but if the main subject is to one side (centre picture) the camera will focus on the background. To overcome this you have to establish focus with the subject in the centre of the frame, and lock it while you compose the picture as you wish (bottom).

This facility is available on certain 110 pocket cameras, compacts and instant picture cameras, and a modified kind has just been introduced on some single-lens reflexes.

There are three systems in use: 'Visitronic', which is an electromechanical version of the ordinary rangefinder; 'Sonar', which sends out a sound signal and measures the length of time it takes to return (devised by Polaroid and used on the SX-70), and infra-red, in which the distance to the subject is computed from the angle at which an infra-red light beam emitted from the viewfinder returns to a sensor placed nearby.

Is all this automation really necessary? It certainly makes things quicker, and this in turn may mean that you can get pictures you might otherwise miss. But people who become interested in making photographs other than snaps for the family album often find that automation can actually restrict their photographic skill.

It is to overcome this problem that manufacturers of automatic exposure cameras have introduced two further refinements on some models. One of these is an automatic exposure compensation facility, which sounds complicated but simply means that you can manually alter the metered setting if you want to achieve a special effect by deliberate over or under exposure. The other is a facility for full manual override, which means that you can switch off the automation when you want to and do the whole thing manually. In many cameras you can still use the built-in light meter, even if you intend to override the readings.

Instant photography

Instant photography is one of the fastest developing branches of the industry. Polaroid were unchallenged in the field for many years, having pioneered the system invented by Dr Edwin Land (who gave his name to the Polaroid Land cameras), and in some quarters their name is still synonymous with instant picture photography. But Kodak are now also in contention, and other systems are on their way.

Instant prints cannot match the conventionally processed kind for quality—at least, not yet. Therefore they are mainly useful for occasions when speed is the important factor, e.g. when you want to photograph guests at a party. In these circumstances they often help to stimulate jollity, and the guests can be given photographs of themselves before they go home. They are also useful for straightforward record purposes in

other fields. For example, estate agents often take instant prints of properties they are advertising.

Perhaps the most serious use of instant photography is in professional studios, where lighting arrangements and overall composition can be checked visually before the definitive series of photographs is taken. This is sometimes done by means of a Polaroid film back on a large-format SLR.

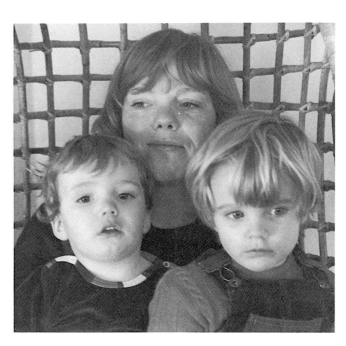

Kodak instant prints are rectangular in format, giving the photographer the choice of horizontal or vertical composition (left and above left). Print size is 6.5 × 9cm (2½ × 3½in); the prints shown here are actual size, although when delivered from the camera they also have a generous white border and a hard-wearing finish. Copy prints or enlargements can be made, although there is no negative.

Polaroid SX-70 prints (above, actual size) measure 8.5 × 8.5cm (3¼ × 3¼in) and are square. They are also hard-wearing, the colours are resistant to fading and, like Kodak prints, they have a good border and can be copied or enlarged.

The Kodak EK160 is the simplest in the range of Kodak instant picture cameras. It has a fixed-focus lens and exposure control is fully automatic so there is nothing to adjust—it is a 'point and shoot' camera. However, there is a lighten/darken control which is useful in certain situations—for instance you often get better seaside pictures if you darken (underexpose) them a little, and pictures in which there is a lot of sky may benefit from being slightly lightened (over-exposed).

Slightly more advanced than the EK160 is the Kodak EK160-EF, which has all the same basic features but with the addition of a built-in electronic flash unit. You switch this unit on simply by sliding it out—the camera adjusts the exposure automatically. All the Kodak instant picture cameras described here incorporate a motor which, after each exposure, delivers a colour print in the rectangular format illustrated on the opposite page.

Polaroid have developed an extensive range of instant picture cameras; the two illustrated here are of the SX-70 type, which is supplanting the earlier peel-apart system; these are, in fact, single-lens reflexes which fold away into an extremely compact package when not in use. The perforated disc visible on the above model is part of the Sonar AutoFocus mechanism by which the lens is focused automatically on the subject at the moment the shutter is released. SX-70 film packs are supplied with built-in batteries, so the photographer need not worry about the possibility of battery failure, and they produce square prints (see opposite page). Other accessories available include flash, either as bulb flash bars or as electronic flash units (see the Model 2 below), supplementary lenses for close-up and telephoto work, a self timer, a remote shutter release button, a special album for displaying SX-70 prints, and various carrying cases.

The most sophisticated Kodak instant picture camera to date is the EK260-EF, which in addition to all the facilities offered by the other two cameras has a lens with a special setting for close-up photography. Selection is by means of a sliding button: in one position the lens is focused on objects 60-120cm (about 2-4ft) from the camera, and in the other on objects at a distance of 120cm (4ft) to infinity.

Your new camera — put it through its paces

Learning to use a camera with assurance takes time: there is no substitute for experience. It is like learning to play the piano or drive a car—books can tell you how to do it, experts can often give valuable guidance and hints, but no one will master any of these activities without getting in there and *doing* it.

Loading

The procedure for loading 110 and 126 cartridges into the camera is simple. That, after all, is why they came into existence in the first place. Open the camera back, insert the cartridge, close the camera back and wind the film on so that the first frame is ready for exposure. Set the film speed if this has to be done manually (although in all probability it will be done automatically by notches in the plastic cartridge).

Loading 35mm cassettes is slightly more complicated, but not much. The rewind knob has to be raised before the cassette can be inserted, then it is lowered again. The end of the leader (the length of trimmed film) is slotted into a fixed spool and the film wound on until the sprocket wheel grips the perforations. Close the back and wind the film on (shooting one or two blank frames) until the counter indicates frame No. 1. Do not forget to set the film speed.

With non-reflex viewing systems make sure that the lens cap is removed before any pictures are taken.

Watch the rewind knob when you wind on the film. If you have loaded

Below: loading a 35mm cassette. The trimmed 'leader' must be inserted firmly into the take-up spool, and is then wound on (the shutter being released as necessary) until the teeth on the sprocket wheel grip the perforations in the film. The back should then be closed and one or two blank frames shot to make sure that the first exposures are not made on fogged film.

Above: holding a camera. Top and centre left—the normal way of holding a camera steady when framing shots horizontally and vertically; bottom left—one way of gaining extra stability if you need to use a slow shutter speed; top right—another alternative, useful where there is no convenient wall; bottom right—a highly stable position, but camera angle is not always suitable.

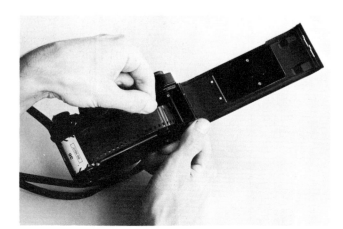

it correctly the knob will turn back-wards (although not necessarily every time, because there is often some slack that has to be taken up first).

Cameras taking 120 film do not have a single standardized loading system, but the basic procedure consists of attaching the paper leader to a take-up spool and winding the film on. With large-format SLRs the film is loaded into a magazine which in turn is fitted to the back of the camera body; with TLRs the film is loaded directly into the camera.

The 35mm cassette is the only one of these that has to be rewound after use and before being unloaded.

Holding the camera

Both hands should be used for maxi-mum stability in hand-held photo-graphy. When standing keep the feet apart, but not exaggeratedly so. If slow shutter speeds are necessary and you do not have a tripod, lean against something firm such as a wall or a stout tree, and position yourself so that your arms are either resting against your body or your elbows are on a solid surface.

The viewfinder

What you will see in the viewfinder depends on the design of your camera. It is common for 35mm SLR viewfinders to show less than will actually appear on the film—usually about 95% of the area. Take some test photographs with objects just outside the viewfinder area so that you can get used to the discrepancy, or you will tend to get unwanted clutter at the edges of pictures.

Using a new camera

Whatever camera you have, try to put it through its paces thoroughly before you start to use it seriously. Use it empty until you have got the feel of it, then with one or two black and white films. Test everything, every feature—closest focusing, delayed action shutter release, various permutations of aperture and shutter speed, the dimmest conditions in which you can get an exposure reading, and so on. This is not only to ensure that it is all working, it is also to develop your own awareness of the camera's performance limits, so that you do not neglect its full potential. Have the films developed and contact

printed. (Contact prints are same size prints made in direct contact with the negatives; they are too small for display purposes but are economical and can be closely analyzed for faults.)

Always examine newly returned films with a ruthlessly self-critical eye, asking yourself if each picture could be better, and how . . . or is it perfect? Then you can begin to anticipate the pitfalls, to identify shortcomings before the exposure is made and the subject gone. You will begin to see the subtle but significant qualities that make the difference between best

and second best—the originality that makes an arresting picture out of a banal subject, a new viewpoint that presents in a different light the things you have seen countless times before. The potential of photography to surprise is limitless.

The viewfinder of a single-lens reflex often shows less than the actual image area, and you need to be aware of this when framing a picture. Although important detail appears to have been cut off in the viewfinder (indicated by the dotted line) it was present on the negative; the print was made from the entire negative area.

Lenses and focusing

Many simple cameras have fixed-focus lenses and these cannot be adjusted by the user. Instead they are set in the factory to give a reasonably well-defined picture of subjects at any distance from a specified minimum—usually about 2m (6ft)—right up to the horizon and beyond.

On other cameras you have to adjust the lens in such a way that the subject comes out sharp rather than as a meaningless blur. A focusing lens is therefore equipped with some means of indicating what distance it is focused on. This is usually either a set of symbols or a scale showing metres and/or feet. The relevant symbol or measurement is aligned with a fixed mark on the camera body or lens, and everything at that distance from the photographer should be in focus; but if the lens is incorrectly set the pictures will have that characteristic woolliness that everyone has seen at one time or another.

Many 110 pocket cameras and compacts have fixed-focus lenses, but some have zone symbols and a few have a distance scale. The lens on most other cameras is focused by means of a rotating ring on the front.

How do you find out the distance between camera and subject? The zone symbol method presupposes that given types of subject will always tend to be about the same distance from the camera, and for most purposes this is accurate enough. Distance scales are even more accurate, but distances are very difficult to judge by guesswork alone.

Two optical systems are in common use to overcome this difficulty. Viewfinder cameras often have a built-in *rangefinder*, and single-lens reflexes a *focusing screen*. The rangefinder system is quick and simple to use. When you look in the viewfinder you see an area with a double image. Adjust the rangefinder until the images coincide, then you can read off the precise distance and transfer it to the focusing ring. More common than this nowadays is the coupled range-

finder, in which the double image is adjusted by the movement of the focusing ring itself: thus the images are only superimposed when the lens (not just the rangefinder) is set to the correct distance.

Focusing a single-lens reflex is somewhat simpler in principle, since you are actually viewing through the picture-taking lens. You see straight away whether the image is in focus or not, and adjusting the lens is not very different from focusing a pair of binoculars. The difference is that light

from the lens has to travel round several angles to reach the eyepiece, and there is some loss of brightness on the way. So for really critical focusing these cameras are fitted with a focusing screen—a special rectancle of glass, seen through the viewfinder, with a circle in the centre. Any vertical straight line on the subject passing through the central circle appears broken until it is exactly in focus. (There are other types of focusing screen, but the one illustrated here is the commonest.)

Left: this is what you can expect to see in the viewfinder of a typical single-lens reflex. When the lens is incorrectly focused (top) the image lacks sharpness and fine detail is lost, while any straight line passing through the central circle is broken as shown. The fragments move further apart if the focusing ring is turned the wrong way and come closer together as exact focusing is approached; when it is exactly right the line is continuous as in the lower picture.

Above: focusing has to be very precise when the subject is close to the camera. In the case of portraits, whether of animals or people, focus on the eyes if possible: it would have been a mistake here to focus on the dog's nose.

Above: a pin-sharp subject against a totally blurred background nearly always makes a successful picture, but is not always easy to achieve.

Below: diagram illustrating how the distance between lens and film plane controls what is in focus and what is not. When the lens is closest to the film, distant objects will be in focus; as the lens is moved away from the film distant objects 'dissolve' and progressively nearer objects acquire sharp outlines.

Lens aperture

Cameras with fixed-focus lenses and no exposure controls are capable of giving good results in average conditions—the key word here being 'average'. As far as camera manufacturers are concerned 'average' lighting is what prevails out of doors on clear days between around 10am and 4pm in summer (with the camera not pointing into the sun).

The logic of this is that many pocket camera owners rarely if ever think about taking photographs except when they are on holiday. When it comes to pictures of children playing on the beach, or of the family admiring some monument or event, camera designers reason—perhaps with a hint of wishful thinking—that it will probably be a fine summer's day, or at least not a rainy one. And when the weather obliges the resulting pictures are likely to be excellent. If it is dull and overcast you will still get pictures, but they will tend to be somewhat murky and to lack that brilliance and sparkle displayed by photographs taken in fine conditions.

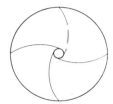

Sometimes the murkiness of the picture may seem to be out of all proportion to the dullness of the day when it was taken. But remember that the human eye has an iris that opens and closes in response to the brightness of the light—look into a person's eye by dim artificial light and the chances are that the pupil will be widely dilated; in brilliant sunshine it will be closed down almost to pinhole size to ensure that not too much light enters. If the eye did not adapt in this way, a clear image would only be transmitted to the brain in one fixed set of lighting conditions. So it is with the non-adjustable cameras, which have no iris to open up in gloomy weather and close down in the sun: you get either a dark (underexposed) picture or, less often, a pale and washed out (overexposed) one.

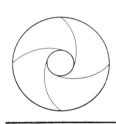

It is obvious, therefore, that one way of making a camera more adaptable is to equip the lens with an adjustable diaphragm similar to the iris of the human eye. In low light the

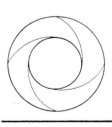

Above: the use of a wide aperture has made photography possible inside a dim barn. Note how normal daylight has burned out detail in the windows.

Opposite page: this sequence of photographs, each displaying approximately the same overall density, shows how correctly exposed pictures are obtained in varying light levels by means of opening or closing the lens aperture. At first glance the difference between the conditions is not especially striking; yet the top picture was taken in harsh sun, the second in overcast but bright conditions, the third under a heavy dark cloud layer, and the last in the dimmest light of all—that of ordinary domestic lamps.

Below: snow scenes can be very bright and a small aperture may be needed if detail is to be kept in the snow.

photographer can choose a large aperture and in bright light a small one, so that the light falling on the film will always be of the same intensity. Light flows through the lens into the camera in much the same way as water flows through a tap into a basin; the more open the tap (or the wider the lens aperture), the greater the flow of water (or light).

Lens aperture is usually adjusted by a ring on the lens barrel which is engraved with a series of numbers, typically 2, 2.8, 4, 5.6, 8, 11 and 16, although the series may be longer or shorter. The step between these numbers is known as a *stop*, or sometimes as an *f/stop*. The higher the

number, the smaller the lens aperture.

The technically-minded may be interested to know how the above series of figures is arrived at. There are two pieces of information you need to have about a lens: its focal length and its maximum aperture; both of these are normally marked on the lens itself. Focal length is the distance (usually in millimetres) between the film and the lens when it is focused on infinity. Maximum aperture is the diameter of the lens diaphragm when this is opened to its fullest extent. Focal length divided by aperture yields the f/number. Most aperture controls proceed in a series of click stops, each corresponding to a number on the scale given above. Thus when a lens of 50mm focal length is set at f/8, the diameter of the opening is 6·25mm, or 50mm divided by 8. It should be added that these figures are not really important, at least to the majority of camera owners; they are given here merely in order to explain what may otherwise appear to be a rather curious and confusing set of numbers. As stated before, the important thing to remember is that if it clouds over, or you wish to take photographs indoors or as night begins to fall you can compensate for the failing light level by choosing larger and larger lens apertures, denoted by lower and lower f/numbers.

Shutter speed

On the preceding two pages it is explained how you can regulate the amount of light that enters a camera by making the lens aperture larger or smaller. Adjustable cameras are equipped with another means of doing the same job—the shutter speed control. Many of the basic models do not have this facility, being set for a fixed exposure time—often of around 1/80 second. But this speed is suitable for only one set of conditions —the average ones described on page 32 (although it is true that some pocket cameras combine a fixed shutter speed with variable aperture control, so that they can be used in a wider range of situations).

The effect of light on photographic film is cumulative. In other words, rays of light start to act chemically on the film from the moment they enter the camera, and continue to work on it until they are shut out again. Then the film has no further contact with any light whatsoever until it has been processed and is no longer sensitive to light.

In the early days of photography glass plates were used instead of the flexible film used today, and they were coated with a relatively crude light-sensitive substance—so crude, in fact, that it took a very long time for the image to register on the plate, and exposures were calculated in minutes rather than fractions of a second. There was no shutter release mechanism as such: the photographer simply removed the lens cap and put it back on when time was up. The films used today are affected so quickly by the light falling on them that much shorter exposures are usually necessary, and it is vital to get the exposure

Compare these photographs with the ones reproduced on page 32; here the duration of the exposure, as well as the lens aperture, has been used to control the appearance of the final prints. Again the overall density of the pictures is similar, showing that in each case the same quantity of light has been allowed to reach the film; but the degrees of movement recorded reveal that shutter speeds were progressively slower from the top picture to the bottom one.

f/4

1/500

f/5.6

1/250

f/11

1/60

f/16

1/30

time absolutely accurate. The exposures are certainly far too short to be within human control, and so modern cameras are equipped with a mechanically timed shutter.

A water tap turned full on may fill a basin in a matter of seconds. But if the flow is reduced to a trickle the process will take much longer—perhaps an hour or more, and several hours if the tap is just dripping. Either way the result is the same: a basin full of water. Similarly, bright sunlight falling on photographic film may create an image in an almost unbelievably brief instant—perhaps 1/1000 second, whereas in that space of time the effect on the same film of faint light such as candlelight may be virtually indiscernible. But allow candlelight to shine into the camera for much longer—say 1/15 second, which is

about sixty-six times as long—and enough light can accumulate on the film to yield a properly exposed picture.

Adjustable cameras therefore have variable shutter speeds, usually in the following sequence: 1 second, 1/2, 1/4, 1/8, 1/15, 1/30, 1/60, 1/125, 1/250, 1/500 and 1/1000 second. The range varies from model to model, some advanced cameras being geared for exposures of up to 10 seconds or more and down to 1/2000. In most cases the sequence will also have a 'B' setting below the longest mechanically set time. When set at B the shutter will remain open for as long as the shutter release button is kept depressed: this gives you the flexibility to make long exposures of minutes or even hours—way beyond the range of mechanically controlled operation (although

you will need a cable release with a locking screw, so as not to have to stand there with your finger on the button for the duration of the exposure). As will be explained later, this comes in useful if you want to make time exposures of the stars wheeling round in the night sky, or of landscapes lit by the moon, to give just two examples.

The success of this photograph lies in the skilful choice of shutter speed: 1/60 second was enough to arrest the motion of the canoeist while allowing the cascading torrents of water to record as patterns of blurred streaks. Shutter speed can be used creatively—it is not just an alternative method of exposure control. However, if your camera does not have variable shutter speeds it may well be set at a speed of around 1/80 second, which would give a picture not very different from this one.

Correct exposure

With non-adjustable cameras there is only one way to guarantee correct exposure every time: that is to photograph only subjects in lighting conditions compatible with the fixed settings of the camera. In other words, instead of adjusting the camera to accommodate the prevailing conditions, you suit the conditions to the camera, or there is no photograph. The manufacturer's instruction leaflet will give you specific indications as to what these conditions are, but usually such basic cameras are set to yield well-exposed pictures in the summer sun, or indoors with flash, which on the whole is where they are most often used. Prospective camera buyers can therefore note that if they wish to take photographs in a wider range of conditions these most basic models will prove to be inadequate for their needs.

One step up from the basic cameras are the pocket cameras and compacts which have a series of symbols—usually three or five—representing different weather conditions. When the user selects one of these symbols he is in effect altering either the lens aperture or the shutter speed (more often the former, although it depends on the camera design), and thus regulating the amount of light that gets into the camera. Weather symbols are a great blessing for those who have no head for numbers but who are nevertheless not prepared to accept the limitations of the non-adjustable camera, yet it must be admitted that they do not give the

So far in this book it has been assumed for simplicity's sake that a correctly exposed photograph is one in which light and dark areas are about evenly balanced, but this is not necessarily the case. When assessing correct exposure you should consider the conditions rather than the subject alone. The seed head above right was held up in direct sunlight against a shaded background, and the camera was set for the sun, not for shade—this is why the background is so dense. A similar setting was used for the picture on the right, but it is easy to see how much lighter this picture is overall—although still correctly exposed.

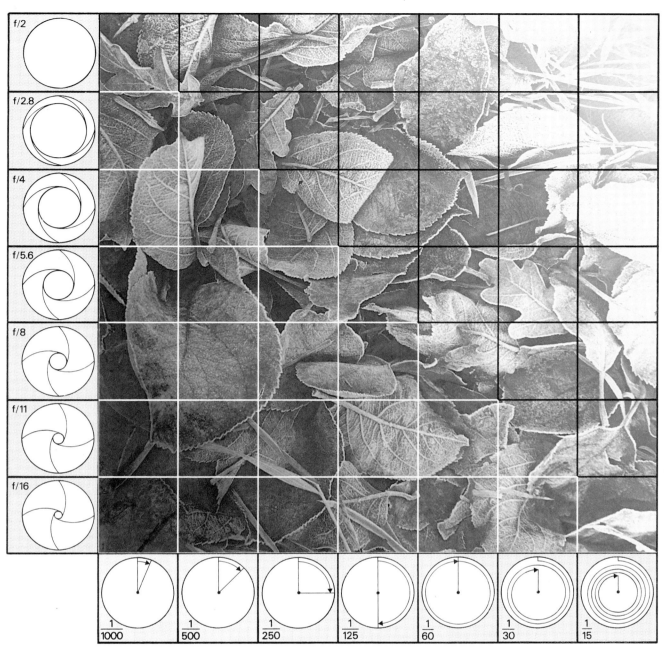

The aperture diagram column (left to right labels): f/2, f/2.8, f/4, f/5.6, f/8, f/11, f/16

The shutter speed dials (bottom, left to right): 1/1000, 1/500, 1/250, 1/125, 1/60, 1/30, 1/15

Aperture and shutter speed working together: this picture may be read like a graph. It is correctly exposed on the diagonal from top left to bottom right: any combination on this line gives the same exposure. Straying from it causes either progressively severe underexposure (towards top and right) or over-exposure (towards bottom and left).

photographer the same degree of really fine control over his images as can be obtained by using the numerical values.

The exposure given for any picture depends on two factors already discussed: lens aperture and shutter speed. Exposure value is computed

from the *volume* of light passing through the lens—controlled by its aperture—and the *time* for which it is permitted to pass through—controlled by shutter speed. The fact that there are effectively two ways of controlling exposure introduces a large but subtle measure of flexibility into the business of taking photographs. The important point to make here is that in many cases there will be a number of permutations of these elements all of which may be 'correct' inasmuch as they all introduce exactly the same quantity of light into the camera.

The respective scales are so designed that the step between

adjacent settings always alters the exposure value by the same amount—by either doubling or halving it, according to whether you open up or close down one stop. This means that once you have worked out one correct combination of aperture and shutter speed, you can alter either of these settings by one or more stops provided that you alter the other one to compensate. For example, a picture that requires an exposure of 1/125 second at f/5.6 will also be correctly exposed at 1/250 and f/4, at 1/500 and f/2.8, or, moving in the other direction, at 1/60 and f/8, or 1/30 and f/16, or 1/15 and f/22. This is called reciprocity.

Depth of field — more about focusing

The term 'depth of field' refers to the area of a picture within which all parts of the subject are in reasonably sharp focus. Compare the photographs reproduced on this page: in one of them everything is sharp, from the nearest object to the furthest; in the other only a single plane is in focus, both foreground and background being blurred and fuzzy, increasingly so with distance from the main subject. The first picture can be said to have great depth of field, the second to have shallow depth of field. This aspect of picture sharpness can be very precisely controlled within certain limits, although only if you have a focusing lens.

There are three factors which control depth of field: (1) the lens aperture; (2) distance from camera to subject, and (3) the focal length of the lens. This last consideration is only relevant to cameras with interchangeable lens systems; the first two are of interest to the owners of adjustable cameras, however simple.

The first factor to consider is lens aperture. There is no need to go into the optical laws governing the behaviour of light as it passes through a lens—that is a rather complicated affair, even though the effects in photographic terms are quite easy to grasp. All the photographer needs to remember is that when a lens is set to its smallest aperture (at its highest f/number) depth of field will be at its greatest; conversely, if a wide aperture (low f/number) is selected, depth of field will be minimized.

The next important factor is subject distance: the closer your subject is to the camera the shallower will the area

of sharpness be; as you focus on objects progressively further away, so the zone of sharp focus increases.

Of course these two factors must always be taken into account together, as they compound or counteract each other. By combining a wide open aperture with the closest focusing distance your camera will allow—say f/2 at 0·5m—you reduce depth of field to just a couple of centimetres. This can sometimes be turned to advantage, but it does mean that focusing has to be absolutely accurate. As you reduce the lens aperture more of the subject will

become sharp, both in front of and behind the precise plane of focus (more behind it than in front) although at close range the difference may not seem to be very great. But as you focus on more distant objects the gain in depth of field becomes rapidly more noticeable, until at f/16, with the camera focused on a point 5 metres away, depth of field will extend from 2·5 metres to the horizon and beyond (infinity, or ∞ in photographic language).

Depth of field can be assessed by the use of a scale which is usually engraved on any focusing lens,

This pair of photographs shows how depth of field is affected by alteration of the lens aperture (both were taken with a standard 50mm lens on a single-lens reflex, focusing on the figure behind the hedge). The top picture was taken at f/16, and everything is in focus from front to back. In the lower picture, taken at f/2, the foreground and background are out of focus, isolating the figure (the tree trunk is also sharp as it is the same distance from the camera).

and/or by the use of a preview button in the case of most single-lens reflex cameras. The scale consists of a series of numbers corresponding to the f/numbers, each of which is marked twice. The two distance values on the focusing ring which fall opposite the two numbers corresponding to the aperture in use represent the nearest and furthest limits of sharp focus. If that sounds complicated—and it certainly takes some getting used to—perhaps an example will help.

The camera is focused at approximately 3 metres (10ft). If the aperture ring is set at f/16, everything from about 2m (6½ft) to infinity will be in focus; if it is set at f/4 the depth of field will be considerably reduced, extending from about 2·6 to 3·5 metres—as indicated by the two figure 4s.

Now suppose the camera is focused on a person's face at a distance of just 1 metre. In this example, at f/16 depth of field would extend from just below 90cm up to 1·2 metres—a total of around 30cm which is a large enough area to contain a person's face and head. But at f/2 depth of field would only be about 5cm, which is so small that you could not get the whole head in focus and you would have to select the most important part (the eyes, in the case of portraits).

The depth of field preview button fitted to many single-lens reflex cameras is a way of manually activating the diaphragm (which is normally done automatically at the moment the shutter is released) so that you can assess the depth of field simply by looking at what is in focus and what is not. This is easier than juggling with numbers.

The three photographs on the right demonstrate how depth of field alters with focusing distance as well as lens aperture. The top picture was taken with the lens set to its smallest aperture (f/16) and sharpness extends from front to back. The picture in the centre was taken with the lens still focused on the buildings but with the aperture opened up to f/2: the reduced zone of sharpness no longer includes the hedge and tree trunk. For the bottom picture the aperture was left at f/2 while the lens was focused on the tree trunk: this is now in focus while the buildings have lost all detail.

Depth of field (continued)

The other factor affecting depth of field is the focal length of the lens you are using. The examples given above are for the standard 50mm lens fitted to many (but by no means all) 35mm cameras. If you use a lens of a longer focal length (a telephoto lens) depth of field will be reduced—such lenses therefore have to be focused very carefully. The opposite is the case with lenses of less than 50mm focal length (known as wide-angle lenses) which give increased depth of field, and which in many circum-

stances do not require such precise focusing for that reason.

So much for the theory. How can you make use of the depth of field phenomenon in practice? When you go out with your camera you will often not need to worry about it at all: many subjects tend to be in the middle distance where even the use of a wide aperture will not prevent the entire scene from being sharp if the lens is correctly focused. But if you are including anything in the foreground you can decide whether or

not you want it to be in focus: a framework of out-of-focus leaves, for example, can make a very attractive

Outside the limits of depth of field, sharpness deteriorates progressively, not all at once. Below: in these pictures of autumn leaves caught in a fence the background to both is out of focus—slightly so at f/16 (left) and markedly so at f/2 (right).

Bottom: this picture, taken from very close, is sharp only in the plane of the hedgehog's eye; beyond that the quills begin to fall out of focus and in the background detail is completely indecipherable.

Depth of field is increased with wide-angle lenses and diminished with telephoto lenses. The photograph on the left was taken with a very wide-angle lens—one of 20mm focal length on a 35mm camera—and depth of field extends from less than 1m (3ft) to infinity.

Below: to obtain the deepest possible zone of sharpness using a standard lens, a small aperture (f/16) was selected and the camera was focused on the pile of logs, because depth of field extends behind the point focused on than in front of it. In this case it extends from about 3m (10ft) to infinity. At their nearer ends the bars of the gate are not within this zone and are technically out of focus, but the blurring is so slight as to be almost undetectable.

setting for a portrait—therefore you move close to the leaves, choose a wide aperture, and focus on the subject.

Perhaps you would like to take a picture through a window with the window frame as well as the subject in sharp focus—then you step back from the window as far as your picture composition will allow, choose the smallest aperture you can, and by using either the depth of field scale or preview button check that both window frame and subject are within the depth of field.

You can use a wide aperture with a reasonably close subject and this will throw the background out of focus, reducing it to a blur—again an effective trick for portraits, and also for flowers or for any other subject that cannot be moved away from a distracting background. This technique is known as *differential focus*.

But depth of field can only be controlled within certain limits—its effects cannot be eliminated in all circumstances. Therefore if you are working very close up, even with small apertures focusing will be critical; similarly if the light is dim you may be obliged to use wide open apertures unless you can arrange to use bright light or faster film, or both.

The relationship between telephoto lenses and depth of field is described more fully on pages 138-139.

Film speed — grain and sensitivity to light

Every film you can buy is given a rating which describes its 'speed', or sensitivity to light. Highly sensitive films are called fast films because they need only a very brief exposure to light for the image to form on them. Slow films take longer to react, although in good daylight even a very slow film such as Kodachrome 25 is correctly exposed in around 1/30 second at f/5.6.

The advantages of fast films are: that they can be used for photography in relatively poor light, or with small apertures where good depth of field is vital, or at very fast shutter speeds when you want to 'freeze' the action; also that accurate exposure is less critical than with slower films. Slow films give finer detail and better colour saturation, and although the difference is not always pronounced it is a good general policy to choose a medium to slow film unless there is a special reason for wanting a faster one.

The reason for this is tied up with the quality known as 'grain'. Seen through a magnifying glass, a photograph is revealed to consist of a granular pattern of light and dark or coloured blotches. The faster the speed of a film, the coarser the granular pattern will tend to be—an effect which does not become evident except at relatively high magnifications such as when big enlargements are made or, in the case of slides, when they are projected on to a large screen (both processes being equivalent to looking at the film through a magnifying glass).

The speed of a film is expressed as a number, and there are different systems in common use for evaluating the speed and arriving at that number. Probably the best known system is the ASA (American Standards Association) rating, but many film packages also give a DIN (Deutsche Industrie Normen) rating. The confusing thing about this is that each one is worked out on an entirely different basis: a doubling of the ASA number represents a doubling of film speed, whereas the same interval in the DIN system is represented by the

Above: using a fast film (rated at 400 ASA) enabled the photographer to give this natural history study a very brief exposure, effectively 'freezing' the movement of the clematis seed heads, which were blowing vigorously in the wind.

Left: with a static and contemplative subject such as this landscape, where the photographer's first priority is to retain the maximum amount of detail, a slow film is the best choice. Since there is nothing moving in the picture there is no need to keep the exposure short (as long as a tripod is available), and so a small aperture can be selected to give maximum depth of field. The result is a picture that is full of fine detail and has good contrast and a pleasing texture.

brightness between the deepest shadow and the most brilliant highlight. On a cloudless summer's day when the sun is throwing hard shadows, the contrast created is so harsh that even the human eye cannot cope with it: you can verify this by looking from out of doors into a dim interior and trying to make out fine detail. Photographic film is even less able than the eye to accommodate high contrast, but faster films are better than slow ones; conversely, if the light on the scene you are photographing is flat and even—such as it might be on a cloudy day—using a slow film will help to put contrast into it, so that the tonal range of the finished photograph is not just flat and uninteresting.

To summarize: for most purposes the use of a medium film—one of 200-400 ASA—is advisable as such films are versatile enough for everyday use.

Use a slow film (up to 125 ASA or so) if
   —you are going to want very large detailed prints, or you wish to project transparencies to a large size
   —you need to use a slow shutter speed for motion-blur effects
   —you wish to build up contrast in the scene you are photographing
   —you object to even slight graininess

Use a fast film (400 ASA or more) if
   —you are taking action pictures in poor or variable light
   —you wish to diminish contrast
   —it is vital to have maximum depth of field
   —you need to work fast and cannot always be sure of getting the exposure right

It will be clear that you may occasionally have requirements that are incompatible with each other—for example, you cannot expect to take sports photos in dim light and then get huge, grain-free prints made from them. But the films that are available will satisfy all but the most exacting photographer.

Finally, do not forget to set the film speed dial on your camera every time you load a new film, unless this is done automatically as it is with certain cartridge-loading cameras.

Above: a different example of the usefulness of fast film—this time not to arrest movement, but to make photography possible in poor light. One property of faster films that becomes increasingly noticeable at high magnifications is grain: it is this that accounts for the salt-and-pepper effect that is particularly evident in the mid-grey areas of this photograph.

Right: Kodak Recording film, one of the fastest generally available films, is rated at 1000 ASA. The results can be very grainy indeed, with harsh, aggressive contrast; however it can be indispensable in very dim light.

addition of 3. Compare the following scale:

25	50	64	125	200	400	1600	ASA
15	18	19	22	24	27	33	DIN

It helps to adopt one of these systems and stick to it; in this book the ASA system is adopted, as on the whole it is easier to use.

Another quality that is affected by film speed is contrast—the range of

Types of film

Films are differentiated according to the following properties:
Format
Speed
Whether they are for colour or black and white pictures
Number of exposures per roll
Whether they are for prints or slides
Whether they are for daylight or tungsten lighting (colour only)
Brand

Format

This is dictated by the type of camera you have. No modern camera takes more than one format, although in some cases it is possible to vary the framing on 120 film to give the photographer the choice of square or rectangular format.

Speed

In general the more basic the type of camera, the fewer film speeds there are to choose from. However, even with 110 format there is a choice of speeds with colour negative films. The range available to the 35mm user is vast, in both black and white and colour. (See pages 42-43.)

Colour or black and white

Any modern camera can be used for either colour or black and white photography. In the case of the 110 format the choice of black and white film is restricted to a single one (Kodak Verichrome Pan) because these cameras are nearly always used for colour prints. The 126 format is also mostly used for colour prints.

You always have to choose films according both to the camera you own and to the facilities you have for viewing or displaying your pictures; all the same, certain subjects are particularly well suited to a given form of presentation. For example, the backlighting that illuminates the rime on the withered plants above would make a stunning subject for a transparency. This is generally true of photographs that rely on spectacular lighting effects or which contain light sources within themselves.

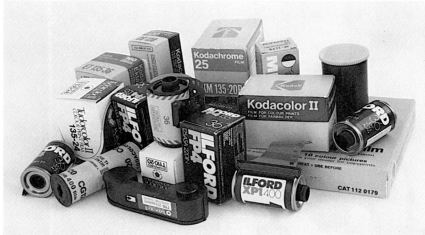

Left: just a few of the films available to the users of popular modern cameras. The range of films found in the shops can be baffling until you are familiar with them.

Black and white enthusiasts use either 35mm or 120 cameras. The word 'Pan' or 'Panchromatic' incorporated in the name of a film indicates that it is sensitive to all the colours of the spectrum, although of course it converts them to various densities of grey. 'Orthochromatic' films are not sensitive to red light and are mostly used for copying.

Number of exposures per roll
This is always stated on the package. It is usually cheaper per frame to buy the longest roll you can, but some people prefer shorter rolls as they have the results sooner.

Prints or slides
The popular colour film market is huge but still expanding, and there is a choice of films for both prints and slides in every format. Colour negative films are for making prints, reversal films are for slides (transparencies). You can have colour prints made from transparencies—at extra cost, of course—and this makes them the more versatile medium. Colour prints can be rephotographed to make transparencies but the quality is not so good. Your choice will probably depend on your viewing system—by whether you prefer to hold slide shows or to pass prints from hand to hand, or put them in an album. There is a 35mm film available for black and white slides: Agfa Dia Direct, a process-paid film.

Daylight or tungsten films
Colour emulsions have to be balanced for the type of light they are to be used in, otherwise the colours look unnatural (see page 54). This is more often a problem with transparencies than with prints. Unless you specify that you want film balanced for tungsten lighting your dealer may assume that you want the daylight type. Tungsten films are not available in the 110 and 126 formats.

Brand
Films from different manufacturers vary in their colour reproduction, as do films made by different processes from the same manufacturer. Therefore when you have found a brand that suits you it is better to stay with it for all your colour photography, otherwise you may notice unexpected and displeasing colour shifts between one film and the next.

Above: print film, most often colour, is more popular than any other type for snapshots taken on holiday or at home. Both black and white and colour print films are available in all the popular formats, and the printing process has the additional advantage that good prints can sometimes be coaxed from less than perfect negatives.

Right: another good subject for a print, but of a more ambitious sort: a black and white picture such as this, with a good tonal range and plenty of interesting detail, could be mounted for hanging on the wall. Black and white photography is rather neglected among amateurs now, but there are a few scenes in which colour is superfluous and which are better represented by a monochromatic image. (See also pages 56-57.)

Lighting — how to use daylight

Light, whether natural or artificial, is a far more versatile and tractable medium than is sometimes supposed. You may not always be able to manipulate natural light at source, but there is a great deal you can do to exploit its qualities or alter them before it reaches your film.

The direction from which your subject is lit is of primary importance. Old-fashioned advice has it that you should always take pictures with the sun over your shoulder. In fact, for most subjects, this is completely wrong: *frontal lighting* of this kind is the flattest and least interesting of all, since it casts little or no shadow to give texture and depth ('modelling') to the picture. Also, people involuntarily screw their eyes up when facing the sun, making faces look uncomfortably distorted.

Lighting from directly *above* and *below* are both difficult to harness for really pleasing results, particularly with people. Both types produce unpleasant pools of darkness which do not flatter the human face. Light from a low angle is the lesser problem because it is rarely found, but the uncritical use of overhead sunlight is all too often the cause of potentially first-rate photographs being spoiled.

Side lighting is more satisfactory for general photography, since it produces modelling shadows that bring out the contours and surface textures of landscapes, buildings or the faces of portrait sitters. The exact angle to choose varies from subject to subject but is usually towards the front rather than behind or at right-angles to it. You cannot, of course, move the sun; if it is in the wrong part of the sky you will have to move your subject or yourself, or both. Where this is not possible, such as with distant views, cities, mountain scenery and so on, try either to work early in the morning or have the patience to wait until the sun is lower in the afternoon sky.

Left: strong lighting from over the photographer's shoulder seldom makes for interesting pictures, but here it has brought out texture in the walls and created strong shadows.

Below left: another example of unpromising light being used to good effect—the overhead sun has been used to create a pool of darkness behind the subject.

Below: a light cloud cover diffuses sunlight and thus lessens contrast. These conditions are ideal for recording fine detail.

Certain subjects benefit from *back-lighting*, which can be somewhat tricky to manage but very effective when it succeeds. Bright light from behind the subject tends to reduce it to a silhouette unless particular care is taken not to underexpose; but fibrous outlines such as those of plants and flowers—and of course girls' hair—take on a radiant, romantic glow. Translucent materials such as thin leaves and flimsy fabric can also be made to shine with a vivid brilliance. Best results with backlighting are often achieved when it is combined with softer lighting from the front, which can be supplied either by a reflecting surface or by the use of fill-in flash (see page 52). Finally, remember to fit a lens hood when you are shooting against the light, unless you are deliberately trying to achieve flare. In this case it may be a good idea to include the light source in the picture, although the effects of this are unpredictable.

Light from whatever angle may be direct or indirect, or a combination of both. Bright direct light such as that from the sun on a cloudless summer's day throws exceptionally hard, dense shadows. The contrast between highlights and shadow areas is then more than film can accommodate, so you have to choose where you want to record detail and expose accordingly. Hard black shadows can be used for striking graphic effects in black and white photography but are usually best avoided in colour. One solution is to place your subjects in the shade—but beware of the shade cast by brightly coloured surfaces which will impart their own hue to the entire scene, with potentially ruinous effects on transparencies.

Another way round this problem is to use a reflector—this need be no more elaborate than a sheet of white paper—to fill in the shadows. If possible, get a helper to hold the reflector and to move it around until you have the effect you want. This may look like rather a pantomime, but it will make a real difference to your photography. A further alternative, as with backlighting, is to use fill-in flash.

A thin layer of cloud will soften

Above left: photographs taken with the camera pointing in the direction of the sun can be very dramatic, with long shadows being thrown out towards the camera. However, a situation such as this requires extremely careful metering, otherwise the picture will tend to be underexposed. With through-the-lens metering, take a reading with the camera pointing away from the direction of the light.

Above: effective photographs can be taken in the highly diffused light caused by mist and fog. Here you should be able to meter the scene normally.

sunlight as well as reducing the blue component of light reflected from the sky. Therefore moderately overcast conditions are particularly favourable to outdoor portraiture and other types of photography where it is desirable to obtain maximum retention of detail and colour fidelity over the entire image area. The cloudier the sky is, the less directional the light becomes; at the same time its intensity eventually becomes so reduced that photography without supplementary lighting may become impossible.

Indoor lighting

It is often possible to take effective photographs indoors using the available light that comes in through doors and windows. Old buildings such as barns and castles are well suited to this treatment because pools of daylight filtering into the dark interiors help to create an atmosphere of age and mystery.

Using window light for other subjects such as portraits is more difficult, although not impossible. It has the advantages that it is free and does not necessitate a change of film or the use of colour-correction filters. Right next to a window the light is at its strongest, but also at its most direct, and therefore contrasty. With increasing distance from the window it gets weaker and softer—preferable for portraits, although you may have to use a tripod so as to be able to use a long enough shutter speed.

Photographing a subject against a window presents similar problems to those which arise with backlighting: you could easily expose for the exterior light by mistake, and end up with a silhouette. Prevent this by placing one or—preferably—two white reflecting surfaces such as sheets (fabric or paper), towels, projection screens or a combination of any of these as close as you can to the subject without letting them intrude into the image area, then take your exposure meter reading from the subject alone. Fill-in flash can also be used. If you are using black and white film you can fill in with ordinary electric light, but do not be tempted to do this with colour transparency film, or your subject will appear to have a nasty attack of jaundice.

Lighting which is mainly or entirely artificial poses other problems, especially if you rely on the incandescent lamps that the average home is equipped with rather than on photofloods or flash. The first of these problems is that of colour balance, which is described in detail on pages 54-55. Another is that a lamp fitted to the ceiling throws awkward shadows that, like those created by noon sunlight, are unflattering to the

48

human face. These lamps are in any case rather dim for photography, and to weaken them further by putting colour-correction filters over the lens means that even with fast films the possibilities are likely to be limited. Replacing domestic lamps with the much brighter photofloods and using Type A film (which is manufactured for use in this type of lighting) is a good solution. Standard and table lamps can be moved around the room until the desired effect is achieved, when the photofloods can be set up in their place. The bulbs get extremely hot and burn out after relatively little use—a few hours or so—so it is economical to save them until you are ready to make the exposure.

Opposite page, top: successful portraits can be taken by window light alone if no other kind is available.

Above left: a lighting set-up that could be used to turn a spare room at home into a photographic studio.

Above: in black and white photography domestic lamps can quite easily be used as the sole light source (although they are less versatile than the much brighter photofloods), or they can be used to supplement daylight, as in this picture. If you mix light sources in colour photography only one of them is likely to be correctly recorded.

Left and opposite: the advantages of using two lights for portrait work. With a single light, the shaded side of the subject's face is lacking in detail. A second light, placed further away than the main source, helps to create a more flattering illumination.

Flash units and how they work

Flash is a special kind of artificial light, with the great advantage that it is portable. There are many units on the market, from simple small ones which offer only a limited quantity of frontal light to large, versatile models offering a high degree of control. The limitation shared by all types of flash is that they are only suitable for close to mid-range work—up to about 10m (30ft) or so in the larger sizes; they are no use for distant objects or landscape work. Among amateurs flash is most often used indoors, although it is also indispensable for certain kinds of outdoor photography.

The two independent systems in common use are bulb flash and electronic flash; the latter is the more recent development and now dominates the market.

Bulb flash takes a variety of different forms, the elements common to all of them being the bulb and the reflector. The bulbs are inexpensive but can only be used once; in the case of flash cubes and flip-flash bars they are supplied ready mounted in individual reflectors which are also discarded once the cube or bar has been completely used up. Most of these are battery powered.

Bulb flash has now largely been superseded by the more sophisticated *electronic flash*. These units have a permanent gas-filled tube which gives an extremely brief but intense flash when an electric current is discharged into it. When the unit is switched on the batteries begin to charge the capacitor—an electronic component which accumulates and stores a high-voltage current. After a few seconds the charge has built up sufficiently to fire the unit, which it does when the circuit is closed through either a synchronizing lead or the 'hot shoe' (the accessory shoe on top of many cameras) at the moment the shutter is released.

The synchronizing lead of an electronic flash unit is plugged into a special socket on the camera marked either with an 'X' or a ⚡ symbol. There may be a similar socket marked 'M' or ℧, which is only for use with

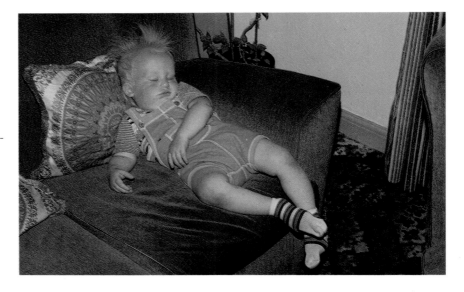

bulb flash. It is *essential* to use the correct socket: electronic flash is more quickly activated than bulbs so the circuit has to be closed at a different point in the shutter releasing cycle, or the picture will be incorrectly lit. If you wish to use the hot shoe instead of a lead check with your camera manual that it is correctly synchronized for the type of unit you are using—it cannot be designed for both.

Some cameras have small electronic flash units built in; this may be convenient for indoor snapshots, but they give the photographer very little control over what he is doing. If you intend to take flash photography seriously, and to use the techniques described later, buy your camera and flash unit separately.

Electronic flash and blue flash bulbs produce a light that is near to noon daylight in colour quality (see page 54). They will tend to override the relatively dim light from household bulbs when used indoors, so normal daylight-type colour films can be used without correction filters.

Camera settings for flash

Whether bulb or electronic flash is being used it is important that the shutter should be fully open when the burst of light reaches its maximum output. Much depends on individual camera design and the maker's manual should be consulted, but if for

Above: electronic flash or a bulb flash unit with blue bulbs can be fitted to the accessory shoe on many cameras, to provide an even frontal light that resembles noon daylight in colour quality. They can therefore be used with normal daylight films.

Below: all popular types of camera are available in versions which have a built-in electronic flash unit. The Agfamatic 2000 is a 110 pocket camera which features such a unit.

Bottom: the Nissin 18M, a reasonably priced yet quite powerful electronic flash unit. Connection to the camera is by the 'hot shoe' (see text) or a synchronizing lead.

3 metres away from the flash. Forty divided by 3 is just over 13, so the correct f/stop is between 11 and 16.

Another example: the guide number (feet) of a unit is 80 for the film being used and the subject is 20ft from the flash. Eighty divided by 20 is 4, so this is the correct aperture setting.

Be careful not to use both metres and feet in the same calculation.

More and more, electronic flash units are being equipped with sensors which measure the amount of light being reflected from the subject, and not the amount being delivered by the tube. When a fixed quantity of

light has been returned the current is cut off, inactivating the flash. With this type of unit the shutter speed and lens aperture settings are constant: the photographer only has to focus the camera and the computer takes care of the rest, determining the duration of the flash accurately within a range extending from about 1/1000th to 1/50,000th second.

If the electronic unit is of the *thyristor* type the full charge of the capacitor is not necessarily exhausted with each exposure, so that the time it takes to recharge (called the recycling time) is shorter, and battery life is preserved.

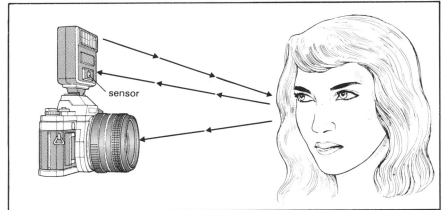

some reason you do not have one, try 1/30 second with bulb flash and 1/60 second or, if there is one, the ⚡ setting with electronic flash. You can use slower speeds, but faster ones are likely to cut off the exposure before the flash has fully illuminated the scene.

Apertures are determined by the *guide number* of the flash unit and the flash-to-subject distance. The guide number system is not really complicated, but it does take some getting used to. In fact, a flash unit does not have one single guide number—it has one for every film speed. The faster the film (or the higher its ASA rating) the higher the guide number. To work out what lens aperture you should use, divide the guide number by the flash-to-subject distance—the manufacturer's table will say whether this should be in metres or feet (some give both).

For example: the guide number (metres) of a given unit is 40 for the film being used and your subject is

Above: diagram illustrating the operation of a computer flash unit: A sensor monitors the light being reflected from the subject; it terminates the flash when the picture is correctly exposed, not simply when the electric charge has been exhausted.

Above left: an actor lit by a computer flash unit held to the left of the camera. The light is fairly crude, throwing hard shadows and flattening out texture in the clothes, but correct average exposure is guaranteed.

Left: the light from a flash unit falls off in intensity very quickly with distance. The child is well lit but the flash has made little impression on the background except where it is reflected directly off the spines of some books.

Further flash techniques

Flash units of any kind are more often than not used on the camera—either built in or fitted to the accessory shoe or, more rarely, large units are fixed to the camera with a flash bracket. Although convenient, this setup has drawbacks. The flat, frontal light it produces is uninteresting because it creates no modelling shadows; at most it causes a deep black line of shadow behind the subject. Faces lit by direct flash acquire an unhealthy pallor and sometimes the eyes glow red like coals—an effect caused by the illumination of the network of tiny blood vessels at the back of the eye.

Therefore, if you buy a separate flash unit, choose one which connects to the camera by a synchronizing lead, and get an extension lead with it. Then you can hold the flash well over to one side or above the camera, or perhaps some distance behind it. Better still, point the unit at the wall or ceiling instead of directly at your subject; this has a softening effect on the brilliant but harsh light that flash produces, and makes it much more flattering, particularly to the human face. When using this technique, which is known as *bounced flash*, in conjunction with the guide number system, work out the flash-to-subject distance via the reflecting surface— i.e. the total distance the light travels— and open up one or two stops more than indicated, according to how

much light you estimate the reflecting surface will absorb. White gloss paint will reflect almost all the light; matt surfaces and darker colours will absorb a lot of it. Experience is the only guide, so do not be discouraged if your first attempts are less than perfect.

The reflector of a computer flash unit can often be swivelled vertically and sometimes laterally too, so that the light can be bounced while the sensor remains pointing at the subject. Operation is still automatic, and the results are excellent even when the flash unit is used from the top-of-the-camera position.

With colour transparency film do not bounce the flash off coloured surfaces because these will tint the entire scene.

Professional photographers often prefer flash to any other kind of light for studio work, because it is both adaptable and predictable—it is not just a feeble substitute for daylight. Professional units may be run from the mains and are therefore not very portable, but similar results can be obtained by the amateur using two or more portable units. A secondary flash unit can be used to fill in hard shadows with a less intense light, or perhaps an extra light is wanted to illuminate the background or to supply backlighting for a model's hair. It is possible to run more than one

unit from the socket on the camera, but a neater solution is to buy an automatic light-sensitive switch called a *slave*, which will react to the main flash by firing off another simultaneously. Any number of units can be combined in this way, each with its own slave unit.

Another alternative is to buy one of the powerful units which has a small fixed flash tube built into it as well as the main swivelling head. This type supplies its own secondary light.

So far it has been assumed that flash is being used as the sole or main source of light. It can, however, perform another very important function known as *fill-in lighting*. If natural light is too contrasty for good results—as direct noon sunlight might be, or when the background is disproportionately bright—flash can be used to open up the shadow areas so that detail in them is not lost. When using flash in this way, meter the scene as you would normally do for an exposure without flash, then close down by about 2 stops—experience is the best guide as to exactly how much you should stop down.

The pictures below were taken on an overcast day. The one on the left was taken without flash; that in the centre was lit by direct flash. But the best result (right) was obtained with flash bounced off a nearby wall, out of the picture and to the right.

Flash can be used to supplement available light: its usefulness is not limited to providing light indoors or at night. Here it has been used as a source of 'fill-in' illumination—in other words it has been used to brighten up an area that was too shadowy to make a pleasing photograph. The skill here lies not in operating a flash unit—anyone can do that—but in recognising the need for fill-in flash in the first place. The photographs were taken in good daylight, which would lead many an unwary photographer to suppose that his pictures could not fail to be properly lit. A fairly small unit is all you need to brighten up the shadows as long as they are not too far from the camera. If you are using an exposure meter, some decrease in exposure value will be necessary to compensate for the additional light: reduce the lens aperture by one or perhaps two stops. Preferably take two or three pictures at different exposures until you are accustomed to using flash for supplementary lighting.

Left: a good example of improvisation. To soften the rather harsh light of an electronic flash unit, the photographer put a polythene bag over it. The diffused light that resulted looks soft and natural.

Far left: a unit such as this has many possibilities. The main head can be pointed in any direction while the sensor remains pointing at the subject, and there is a smaller fixed tube to provide fill-in light.

Colour photography

Colour is such a familiar part of our everyday life that it is tempting to take it for granted in photography, assuming that it will 'come out' in pictures just as we see it in real life. Even if this were the case (and it is not) a bland acceptance of whatever colour happens to be in front of the lens would deprive the photographer of an important creative element because, like nearly everything else in photography, colour can be manipulated or exploited.

A fundamental quality that the photographer needs to be aware of is known as colour temperature. Sunlight is always sunlight, but between dawn and dusk on a given day it may progress through a range of different hues: the pinkish light of dawn (low colour temperature) gives way to a brighter and more neutral light at noon (high colour temperature), and then as the sun sets it may turn to orange or red (low colour temperature

again). Not all days follow the same pattern of course—atmospheric conditions interfere with the sun's light, and there are seasonal variations as well. A white wall, photographed in these different conditions, will have a distinctly different colour cast in each picture, although in life the brain compensates for the variations and perceives a white wall whatever the lighting.

Ordinary incandescent light bulbs give out an orange-yellow light that is quite different from noon sunlight, but again, the brain converts this into 'normal' light so that you are not aware of its colour (unless you switch on a household lamp in broad daylight). The camera, however, isolates this difference in light quality and the photograph presents it to the eye out of its proper context, with the result that it looks completely unnatural.

To overcome this problem you can either use one of the films manu-

factured especially for use in tungsten lighting or, if your camera is already loaded with daylight-type film, use a colour correction filter (see table). The problem with filters is that they necessitate an increase in exposure, and since indoor lighting is usually rather low in any case this may mean that with slower films it just becomes impossible to photograph anything but static subjects.

As an alternative, and to save fiddling about, you can just ignore the unwanted colour quality of the light

Below left: colours found in nature are nearly always appealing, and are perhaps richer in the autumn than at any other season.

Below: there are times when there is little or no colour in the scenery, particularly over water when the sky is overcast but still bright. These conditions are bad for colour photography unless there are bright hues in the subject—this will then stand out against the insipid background.

and go ahead with pictures on your daylight-type film—but try to include the light source as part of the picture. Doing this helps to situate the subject in a context which accounts for its colour bias. But note that this trick does not work the other way round: if you are taking pictures in daylight with a film balanced for tungsten lighting, you need to use a colour correction filter, otherwise the pictures will have a bluish tinge—an effect which is almost always horrible and can seldom be used for a 'creative' effect.

Exploiting colour

The psychological effects of different colours are well enough known to planners and designers and are exploited in various different ways. Red is associated with heat and danger, hence its use to designate hot water taps, live electric cables and so on, and to stop traffic or warn of hazards. Blue is at the opposite end of the colour spectrum and often suggests nocturnal stillness and cold. Between the extremes of the visible spectrum are Nature's colours—green, gold and brown—which can symbolize safety and tranquillity and evoke a wide range of emotional responses.

There are no hard and fast rules, of course. Any one *hue* can appear in many different *tones*: it can be pure and saturated, so that even blue can have an intense brilliance (e.g. the sky in mountainous areas), or it can dwindle into greyness, so that otherwise vivid red, yellow and orange hues become quite muted. And any hue of any tone can be either light or dark.

All this gives the photographer enormous scope to make a variety of colour impressions. A photograph can

Above left: good colour photography does not rely solely on brilliant or contrasting colours. Here there are subtle variations of tone, shade and texture arising from the delicate green hue that is characteristic of woodland in early spring.

Above: the Horse Guards with their bright uniforms and glossy mounts are a natural colour subject. Pageantry, military parades, official occasions—they all use colour to attract notice and create a feeling of national pride and optimism. Colours will therefore be bold but harmonious—which is ideal for photography.

Colour correction filter table

	Daylight film	Tungsten Type A	Tungsten Type B
Candle light	(80A)*	(82C)*	(82C)*
100-watt bulb	80A	82C	82B
Photoflood	80B	No filter	81A
Clear flash	80C	81B	81C
Blue flash	No filter	85	85B
Direct sun	No filter	85	85B
Cloudy sky	81C	85B	Not suitable
Clear blue sky	85C	Not suitable	Not suitable

*Candle light is too low in intensity and colour temperature for any filter/film combination to yield daylight colours. 'Moody' pictures can be obtained using the filters given in the table. If no filter is used the results will be very red.

consist of a single colour in varying tones and levels of brightness; it can consist of mixed colours from adjacent bands of the spectrum and which therefore harmonize, or it can consist of a mixture of totally dissimilar (complementary) colours, in which case it will be lively or agressive —maybe even vulgar.

It pays to consider these factors carefully when composing a picture in which colour plays a vital part, otherwise some of the effects may surprise and displease you. For example, a photo of your family standing in front of an ancient castle could be completely ruined by the inclusion of some anonymous sight-seer in a bright red shirt, because the

viewer's eye automatically fixes on to the red patch, to the detriment of the main subject. Red flowers would have the same effect, particularly if lit by the direct rays of the sun. But if the flowers themselves are the main subject you can harness the same principle to highlight them against a neutral background, thus dramatically increasing the impact of the picture.

No combination of colours, however garish, is so irredeemably violent that it is incapable of yielding a good photograph—provided that the colour is appropriate to the subject. At the same time, effective photographs can be composed of colours so muted that they are almost monochromatic in appearance.

Black and white photography

Not so long ago it could be said that as far as most people were concerned the advantage of black and white photography over colour was one of cost: colour was expensive, and early colour prints especially were not good. But with the proliferation of colour print processing houses that has occurred in recent years and the fierce competition between them for the snapshot market, this has ceased to be true—there is little to choose between the two forms of photography on the grounds of cost alone.

The majority of photographers now take it for granted that colour pictures represent the world more truthfully than monochromatic ones, and in a literal sense they are right. This being so, who uses black and white today, and why?

Professional photographers may be required to work in black and white for technical reasons. An obvious example is the Press photographer whose work will be used in a daily newspaper where colour is not available (and in any case he can get black and white prints to his paper sooner than colour).

People who want to be in complete control of their photography all down the line often work with black and white because it is the more versatile medium. The relative ease with which black and white film can be developed and printed at home brings *every* stage of the photographic process within reach of the amateur—and the cost of setting up a darkroom need not be prohibitive. Many people imagine that the photographer who does his own processing and printing at home does so in order to make a saving on cost; but in fact the enthusiast may sometimes spend more money on materials than he would have had to pay to the commercial printer. He does this for the satisfaction of getting *exactly* the result he wants, instead of just getting a picture that has been mechanically churned out with never a thought being given to the special qualities of the negative in question.

It would be misleading in this case

to suggest that the same never applies to colour: the dedicated photographer can exercise as much control over his colour prints as he can over black and white. But it is a far more complicated, difficult and expensive business and anyone who considers taking it up seriously would be wise to become thoroughly familiar with the black and white process first.

The third category of photographers who choose to work in black and white consists of those who take advantage of its qualities of abstraction to make a different type of image, exploiting compositional devices such as form, texture, line and so on. They 'interpret' the world in their pictures rather than reproducing it as literally as possible; therefore this is often seen by its practitioners as a more creative form of photography.

Of course it is not essential to process and print your own pictures to enjoy black and white photography. Commercial processors will follow any instructions you give them as best they can. When you take a roll of black and white film to the chemist or photo-shop for processing, always ask for a contact sheet and not a complete set of prints. A contact sheet is simply a sheet of photographic paper on which all the negatives are printed in strips, without enlargement. Although individual pictures are small you can examine them through a magnifying glass to decide which ones you want printed and how (i.e. what type of paper surface you prefer and what grade, whether you want the whole negative printed or just part of it, and so on).

Right: the undoctored print made from a 35mm negative is ruined by shapeless branches in the foreground. To obtain the much better picture below, the photographer disposed of the branches by cropping away almost half of the negative area and shielding the top left hand corner in printing. Slight underexposure has helped to make a light and airy 'high key' effect.

Black and white photography lends itself to treatment as an abstract or semi-abstract medium. Above left: this bizarre and even menacing effect was created by powerful searchlights sweeping across the heads of a crowd watching a firework display. Above right: a bold design discovered by an observant photographer—but the subject was nothing more than a number of concrete drainage pipes laid end to end on the ground, ready for installation.

Strong dense lines and shapes are the subject of the photographs below. Both were printed on hard (contrasty) paper to enhance their stark, graphic qualities. Below left: exposing for outdoor light has converted the shapes in the foreground to silhouettes in this striking picture taken at the railway station in Copenhagen. Below right: a simple but carefully balanced composition, the dominant element of which is the hard shadow thrown by a telegraph pole in low direct sun.

Prints or slides — which are better?

If you are new to photography it is worth giving some thought at an early stage to the question of whether slides will suit your needs better than prints, or vice versa. Of course you can choose either type each time you buy a new film, but most people will find it better to specialize as each has its own particular advantages and viewing equipment.

The colour print is undoubtedly the most popular type of photograph in the mass market, and there are very good reasons for this. Processing and printing is now so cheap that colour enprints cost little more than black and white; they are convenient to pass around, carry in a pocket or handbag or put in an album. The negatives are always returned with the enprints so that you can have

further copies made, enlarged if you like. Another good reason is that making prints is a two-stage process: the film is first developed to turn it into a strip of negatives, and each negative is then printed on to paper. Errors of exposure can to a certain extent be compensated for at the printing stage, so with prints you will often get an acceptable picture from a less than perfect negative. Colour balance can also be altered by filtration so that any unwelcome colour cast can be removed. Filters are always used in colour printing in any case—it is just a question of adjusting the relative densities of the filters, which nowadays is often done by computer.

Most laboratories do not charge for unprintable negatives, so you only

have to pay for film processing and the prints you receive.

Different paper surfaces are available, but unless you specify otherwise you will probably be given a matt surface, as this is the most suitable for general purpose photography. For crisp, sparkling photographs where fine detail is important a glossy surface is often preferable; for a more muted effect the matt papers are better.

Colour reversal film is the most adaptable type as it can be rephotographed to make either colour or black and white negatives, or printed down direct on to colour reversal paper. Transparencies can be made from colour negatives, but this is less satisfactory than the reverse procedure. You can have conversions of either type carried out by commercial processing firms.

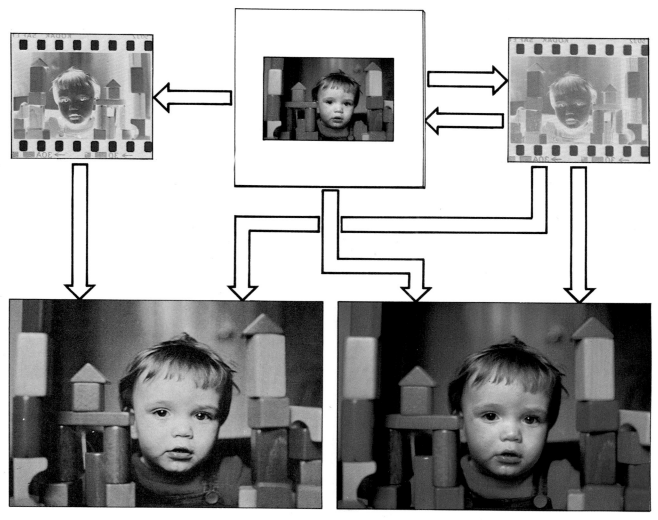

Slides, or transparencies, are an altogether more demanding medium. You cannot really view them without special equipment—a pocket glass at the very least, or a hand-held slide viewer. The drawback with these is that each photograph can only be viewed by one person at a time; also the image is rather small. The alternative—the familiar projector and screen in a darkened room—can be troublesome to set up and expensive to buy in the first place. Furthermore, since transparencies are developed in a single (lengthy) process there is no second chance to compensate for errors in exposure: the finished product consists of exactly the same piece of film as was originally in your camera.

Given such problems and limitations, why bother with transparencies at all? The answer is that for really brilliant, high-quality results there is nothing as dramatic as the projected image. It can reproduce a far greater range of light levels than a print can—the highlights actually shine, the colours jump out of the screen—and so it gives a much more authentic impression of the original scene. Besides this, some people enjoy the sense of occasion and the atmosphere

of the 'slide show' for its own sake.

There are two further points in favour of the transparency. First, you can have prints made, so you get the best of both worlds (although at extra cost). Second, transparencies are always preferred to prints for publication where colour is concerned. If one day you intend to submit pictures to magazine and book publishers you should make this your medium.

To sum up: prints are more convenient and need not involve you in any further cost. Transparencies require more of the photographer in terms of both camera technique and financial outlay, but are ultimately more rewarding. Perhaps it should be added that if you are prepared to pay for the service, you can have beautiful enlargements made from either negatives or transparencies, although for really large pictures, say $40{\cdot}6 \times 50{\cdot}8$cm (16 × 20 inches) the 110 and 126 formats are never as good as 35mm or larger.

It is possible to make black and white transparencies, but this is rather specialized and the paper print is widely regarded as the most satisfactory way of displaying monochrome photographs.

Top: sometimes the subject itself determines how a picture would be best presented. A family event such as a christening is a natural subject for a colour print.

Below: pictures with shining highlights are best when projected. The highlights and light sources then glow just as they did in life; transparency film can also record a greater range of brightness than a print and so will contain more authentic detail.

Left: this portrait would look good as a slide or as a print. The highlights and strong colours would certainly benefit from being projected on to a screen; as a print it would look best on glossy paper because this type can accommodate contrast better than the matt surfaces.

Below: contrast is not excessive, but this picture contains a wealth of fine detail and would make an impressive print, especially at a large size.

Close-up photography

Every combination of camera and lens has a closest focusing distance, as described on pages 30-31. In basic pocket cameras reasonable sharpness begins at about 2m (6ft) away from the camera and this cannot be varied; anything closer than that will appear fuzzy, progressively more so as the subject approaches the camera. More advanced cameras with focusing lenses offer a smaller minimum subject distance—down to perhaps 1m (3ft) in the case of 35mm compacts—while the standard 50mm lens fitted to 35mm SLR and rangefinder cameras can usually focus on objects as little as 30-40cm (12-15in) away.

A lens brings distant objects into focus at a point relatively close behind it and nearby objects at a point much further away: therefore as the camera to subject distance *decreases* so the lens to film plane distance has to *increase*—and in inverse proportion. In practice this means that focusing on widely separated but distant points entails only a minor adjustment of the focusing ring, whereas altering focus by just a few centimetres at close range means turning the ring a long way round, and the forward movement of the lens is very marked indeed. It is the necessity for such large increases in physical length that accounts for the close-focusing limitations of standard lenses.

These limitations can be overcome by the use of supplementary lenses, bellows units or extension tubes, all of which are used in addition to the standard lens. Special close-up or 'macro' lenses are also available, and these are fitted in place of the standard lens. A reversing ring provides yet another alternative.

Supplementary lenses are single-element lenses which are fitted in front of the main lens to make close focusing possible. Their strength is measured in *dioptres*: 1 dioptre is weak and 3 dioptres strong. Two or more supplementary lenses can be used together, although image quality begins to deteriorate.

Extension tubes are fitted between the lens and camera body, introducing the extra distance between lens and film plane that would be too cumbersome to incorporate into standard lenses. They are commonly supplied in sets of three or more and can be used singly or together according to the degree of magnification required. A whole set of three used together will typically give an image at the film plane around three times as large as the original.

Bellows do the same job as extension tubes, but offer continuous (stepless) focusing rather than a series of steps. They enable photographs to be taken from 6cm (2½in) away or even less, giving an image magnified by up to six or seven times. They are also considerably more expensive than extension tubes.

Macro lenses are designed to give optimum image quality in close-up photography, usually giving up to around ten times magnification when used together with bellows, depending on the manufacturer. They are fitted in place of the standard lens and are expensive to buy, but they can be used for normal photography.

A *reversing ring* can be screwed on to the thread at the front of a lens designed to take filters, enabling it to

Left: an inexpensive bellows unit fitted to a 35mm single-lens reflex was used to take these pictures of pinheads. In the top picture the image formed on the negative is exactly life-size; the other three prints show progressively greater degrees of magnification. You could not achieve the same results by enlarging a single negative to different sizes because the image would become degraded by obtrusive grain and a large print would show no more detail than a small one.

Below: extension tubes and a bellows unit; the use of these is described in the main text.

Close-up photography is of particular value to the naturalist. Above: a seed head photographed with a macro lens fitted with ring flash (an electronic flash tube in the form of a ring which surrounds the front element of a lens, used to provide even illumination of a small area). Left and above left: depth of field is very shallow in close-up photography, so it is essential to be able to focus quickly and accurately when photographing insects that may move at any moment.

be attached to the camera body back-to-front. Installed in this way a standard lens offers a limited close-up facility for a modest price.

There are two major problems with close-up photography: measuring the correct exposure and getting adequate depth of field. It is also essential to avoid the framing error caused by parallax.

Since in close-up photography the light reflected from a smaller than usual subject has to be distributed over the normal image area, its intensity will inevitably be reduced and a compensating increase in exposure will be necessary. This can be worked out mathematically, but by far the best solution is to use a camera with through-the-lens metering, which will enable the user to

meter a close-up subject as easily as any other.

The other major problem is with depth of field. We have already seen on pages 38-41 how this is reduced drastically at close focusing distances. In macro work sharpness continues to be compressed into a narrower and narrower band until it exists effectively in a single plane, even at the smallest apertures. Focusing has to be absolutely precise; there is no margin of error in setting camera-to-subject distance. The easiest and most certain way to achieve this degree of accuracy is by single-lens reflex viewing: by actually *seeing* what is in focus and what is not.

A further advantage of SLR viewing is that exact framing and composition of the picture is possible. In systems

where the viewing lens and the taking lens are separate the framing of the scene will always vary between one lens and the other. This disparity (parallax) is imperceptible in normal photography, but marked in close-ups. Once the camera has been focused it must be moved so that the subject is directly in front of the taking lens, but since the exact framing cannot then be optically checked the possibility of bad composition is always present.

It will be obvious from these remarks about exposure, depth of field, parallax and the benefits of being able to fit attachments between lens and camera body that, for the serious enthusiast of close-up photography, the single-lens reflex camera with TTL metering is really the only choice. By all means try a few close-up experiments with other cameras, using any kind of magnifying glass you can fix in front of the lens; but do not be surprised if the results—at least to begin with—are rather unsatisfactory.

Accidental effects, lucky mistakes

By definition, accidental effects cannot be contrived but must be stumbled upon. Once this has happened, however, the photographer can seek to recreate the circumstances of the serendipity and harness the effect to his creative purpose. The more elusive the effect, the more fascinating it becomes and the greater the challenge to try to duplicate it and add it to your range of skills.

Bizarre photographic accidents are more likely to occur with direct vision viewfinder cameras than with single-lens reflexes, for the simple reason that if you view through the taking lens you will be more likely to reject an unexpected trick of the light as being undesirable.

Once the unexpected has been recorded, however inadvertently, it may suggest possible avenues of exploration to the photographer who enjoys experimenting. The photographs reproduced here are examples of such unsolicited special effects.

Below: the effects of flare are rather unpredictable, particularly when a camera without a reflex viewing system is being used. The oddly shaped blobs here are in fact an ordinary case of flare, but the photographer was using an ancient camera with a diaphragm that—surprisingly—was really that shape.

Above: this nocturnal effect occurs particularly in high-contrast situations with automatic exposure control. The resulting composition is powerful and dramatic; but for a more accurate rendering of the scene the exposure would have to be increased—probably by about two stops.

Right: another case of flare. A telephoto lens was being used with a lens hood fitted so that the sun, which is just outside the image area, did not shine directly on to the front element of the lens. Therefore there are none of the characteristic blobs usually associated with flare; instead stray light has spread over the entire image, reducing contrast and altering the colours.

Left: some 35mm cameras have a double (or multiple) exposure facility built in, but this example was achieved by a somewhat different method. The photographer, not noticing that he had reached the end of his film, tried to wind it on normally. However it was securely anchored to the cassette spool, so the sprocket wheel simply tore the perforations. The film remained stationary, but the shutter was cocked for another exposure—and luckily both subjects were similar. It would be better not to do this deliberately.

Right: an extreme case of camera shake. The photographer had last used his camera with its shutter on the B setting, and, anxious to photograph this street scene quickly, raised his camera and shot without checking the exposure settings. During the exposure (probably about $\frac{1}{4}$ second) the pedestrians and cars have continued to move, while camera shake has blurred any fixed objects such as the buildings. The negative was naturally overexposed, but not impossible to print. This was a genuine accident, although some photographers regularly employ this technique when an impressionistic effect is sought.

This phenomenon is very difficult to explain away, nor has the photographer ever succeeded in replicating it. Since the picture was taken with a rangefinder camera and the curious coloured streaks were not noticed by the photographer at the time, it seems reasonable to assume that they were formed in the lens rather than actually existing outside. Or perhaps they were something to do with sunlight refracted by ice crystals suspended in the air—the picture was taken at high altitude in the Swiss Alps. However caused, the effect is beautiful and intriguing—and completely unexpected.

Filters — for more creative control

Filters fall into two categories: those used to alter the colour of the light so that it matches the film being used, and those used for controlled distortion of the light in the pursuit of special effects. There is a degree of overlap between these categories. Some of the filters in the former category are of great value to any photographer; those in the second will appeal to people who enjoy experimenting with light and colour and whose interest is not confined to 'straight' photography.

Filters for black and white photography

Coloured filters when used with black and white film lighten their own colour, making it pale grey to white in the finished print, and darken complementary colours, making them dark grey to black. This is because their effect is to let light of their own colour through while blocking other colours; they do not simply convert all light to their own colour. Mixed hues reproduce as greys of varying density.

The commonest application of this principle is in the darkening of blue skies which, without filtration, will provide a white background against which white clouds simply vanish. (Blue sky comes out white in un-filtered photography because black and white film is sensitive to ultra-violet light, of which there is a lot in sky light, although it is invisible to the human eye.)

To make the clouds stand out, use a yellow, orange or red filter according to the measure of contrast required. The effect of a yellow filter is fairly gentle, that of a red one stark and dramatic; the orange one is somewhere in between.

The main uses of coloured filters with black and white film are as follows:

Yellow: improves landscapes by making grass and foliage slightly paler; enhances the surface texture of snow; slightly darkens sky.

Orange: brings out surface texture of wood, brick and stone; darkens sky more than a yellow filter.

Red: has the same effect as orange, only more so; can give blue sky a stormy or almost nocturnal appearance.

Yellow-green: similar to yellow but the effect is more marked; also useful for outdoor portraits.

Green: makes leaves and grass pale, giving good detail in green landscapes and woodland pictures.

Blue: recommended for indoor portraits with a tungsten light source as it lightens blue eyes and darkens red lips slightly.

Filters for colour photography

Coloured filters are not often useful with colour film as they impart their hue to the entire scene. Occasionally this may make for a striking sunset or a convincing blue seascape etc., but as a general rule the indiscriminate addition of a single colour to a photograph is not advisable. Exceptions are the colour-correction filters used to compensate for mismatching of film with light source (discussed in detail on pages 54-55) and various special effects filters such as the graduated kind (see below).

Above left: green plants tend to grow darker as the year wears on, and can appear in black and white pictures as rather dark, heavy masses. A green filter sometimes helps to 'lift' the lighter shades, introducing more tonal variation into such solid areas.

Opposite page: a cloudy sky often lacks impact in black and white photography. The use of a yellow (top), orange (centre) or red (bottom) filter improves things by increasing contrast and darkening the sky.

Above: graduated filters can be used to introduce colour to one half of suitable pictures. Here a graduated blue filter has been used to intensify the colour of the sky.

Below: filters from the Hoya range. Those with circular mounts are screwed directly on to the front of a lens; they are available in various sizes for lenses of different diameters. Alternatively, a single set of square filters can be used with any lens for which you have a filter holder.

Filters (continued)

Filters for both black and white and colour photography

Ultraviolet, polarizing and neutral density filters are equally useful with either type of film.

Ultraviolet: absorbs light from the ultraviolet part of the spectrum which is invisible to the eye, but which can mar landscapes by introducing distance haze; also has the same effect of darkening the sky as a yellow or orange filter. It has no adverse effects and is therefore often left permanently in place to protect the lens.

Polarizing: used principally to reduce reflected glare. Can have the same effect on black and white film as a yellow or orange filter; can also be used to intensify colours, particularly the blue of the sky. The effect of a polarizing filter varies with its angle, so it has to be rotated while the effects are judged. This can be done with the filter in place on single-lens reflex cameras; with other types it has to be held up to the eye first, and the angle carefully preserved as the filter is positioned on the lens.

An eight-point starburst filter has been used to make the sun the most prominent feature of this morning landscape. The starburst filter can be rotated, so that the points can be arranged as the photographer wishes, and they are available with four, six or eight points. A further variation is that two of them can be used together and rotated independently, so that it is possible to vary the angle between the two sets of points. This type of filter is equally suitable for black and white and colour photography.

Right: polarizing filters can also be used for black and white photography as well as colour. They have two uses: to reduce reflected glare from the surface of water, glass and so on, as in this photograph of water weeds; and to intensify the blue of the sky (grey in black and white photography) with an effect very similar to that of the graduated blue filter illustrated on page 65.

Prism filters divide and repeat the image or a part of it in many different ways. Although this is in keeping with some subjects they should be used sparingly as the effect can get tiring if overworked. They are mostly used for colour photography, although they will also work in black and white.

Neutral density: these filters reduce the overall intensity of light without affecting its colour or other qualities. They are useful when the light is too bright for the film being used, or when either a slow shutter speed is required to create motion blur or a wide aperture to reduce depth of field.

Increasing the exposure

All of the filters mentioned so far except for the ultraviolet one work by reducing the amount of light entering the camera, whether over the entire spectrum or only a part of it. To get a correctly exposed photograph, therefore, an increase in exposure is necessary.

Cameras which have through-the-lens metering, and those with the meter window situated inside the lens mount so that it is covered by any filter that is fitted, meter only the filtered light and will give a reading

that automatically compensates for the light loss. This is not the case with independent metering; the increase in exposure has to be worked out and the exposure controls adjusted accordingly. To enable this to be done, every filter is given a *filter factor* by which the metered exposure must be increased. A factor of × 2 means that the exposure should be doubled (increased by one stop), × 3 indicates a 1½ stop increase (*not* 3 stops!), × 4 a 2 stop increase, and so on.

Special effects filters

These are not really filters at all. Trick lenses might be a more accurate term; however, they are often treated by manufacturers as belonging to their ranges of filters and have come to be known as such. The variety of new special effects filters continuously appearing on the market testifies to the seemingly inexhaustible ingenuity of the makers and to the popularity of this kind of photography. The following is a selection of some of the more useful kinds commonly available; for more detail, consult one of the makers' catalogues.

Soft focus: diffuses the image, giving it a romantic, dreamlike

quality; most often used for portraits of girls. Several types are available, some offering different degrees of diffusion, others a central sharp zone with increasing fuzziness towards the edges, and so on.

Starburst: draws rays of light out from bright highlights so that they become crosses, or stars. Available in four, six or eight-point versions.

Prism: splits the image so that the main subject is repeated one or more times in a linear or circular configuration.

Graduated filters: one half of these is coloured, the colour merging into clear glass in the other half. A graduated blue filter can be used to intensify the blue of the sky without affecting the landscape beneath it; a red one creates an artificial sunset effect, and so on.

There are many more. They can be used on their own or combined, making possible an immense variety of effects. For experimental work with these attachments a single-lens reflex is undoubtedly the best camera to use, because aperture and focal length can alter their effects unpredictably.

Snapshots — don't wait . . . shoot

Photographers are often in danger of taking themselves too seriously. This does not apply to all, of course, but to those whose meticulous attention to technical detail and the finer points of composition may cost them many a good picture when the subject cannot or will not wait for exposure meter readings, precise focusing, artistic filter effects and the like. A photograph taken on impulse, on the spur of the moment, may or may not be properly exposed and in focus — indeed it may be a total write-off. But there is always the chance — and this is especially true when there are people around — that a characteristic gesture, a fleeting moment of spontaneous comedy or a bizarre little incident may be caught for ever by a watchful photographer whose reactions are quick and who is not too pedantic about technical perfection. Such chances, once missed, may be irretrievably lost. Try recreating a funny moment for the camera: the results are almost always stilted, wooden and lacking in spontaneity.

This is not to suggest that it is worth shooting at anything that moves, only that it is better not to be inhibited when an interesting situation develops.

In this type of photography the owners of the most basic pocket cameras and the owners of the most sophisticated automatic cameras have an advantage over all the rest: namely, that there are no controls to set anyway, so no time is wasted.

Adjustable cameras can be preset so that they are ready to cope with

Left and below left: the streets are fertile ground for photographs taken on impulse without too much consideration for technical finesse. It helps if you preset the camera for the conditions as far as possible, and when you see likely-looking picture material don't wait to think about it — shoot at once. For every really good picture there are bound to be some less successful ones, but occasionally you get something so good that it more than makes up for a few disappointments.

most eventualities, and if this is done with care there need hardly be any complete failures, if any at all. First, take a number of exposure meter readings and from these work out an average for the conditions, using a safe shutter speed (i.e. about 1/125 second) and whatever aperture follows from this. Then set the infinity symbol (∞) against the operative f/stop number on the depth of field scale (because you do not need to *focus on* infinity for depth of field to *extend to* infinity). You will then obtain maximum depth of field for the lighting conditions, and the odds on any photograph coming out sharp all over are at their greatest. If you have the choice use a wide-angle lens, as this will extend depth of field even further. (In fact, you would effectively be using your adjustable camera as a fixed-focus camera, duplicating the exposure and focus settings built in to non-adjustable models.) Another way of achieving the same result is to use the exposure tables supplied by the film manufacturer to establish

Left and above: if you see something funny take a picture of it right away —do not worry about composition. You can have superfluous details cropped away when the picture is printed.

Above right: the driver only had to stop the car for a moment for the passenger to take this snapshot through the window.

Below: children can easily lose their look of natural spontaneity unless you work quickly.

results with prints than with transparencies, because minor errors in exposure can be compensated for and pictures can be cropped at the printing stage.

After altering the camera settings for your more considered shots, remember to return them to their snapshot or 'grab shot' positions in readiness for the next unforeseeable incident.

shutter speed and aperture, and to set the focusing ring in the same way as before, ignoring any built-in meter readings. Heretical though it may seem, this can be a most convenient method.

These techniques work better with fast films than with slow, and in colour it is easier to obtain consistently good

Composition — your more considered shots

While there is always an element of intuition in the way a photographer arranges the various elements in his picture, there are nevertheless some simple guidelines which will help the beginner to get more lasting pleasure from his photography. These guidelines can and should be ignored when necessary (e.g. when something happens so suddenly that there is no time to reflect before pressing the shutter release) although it is worth remembering that some of the greatest photographs ever taken combine striking composition with 'event' subjects that did not wait for the photographer. Speed of reaction and compositional flair can be present together in the same photograph.

Basic guidelines

When you look through the view-finder of your camera *examine* what you see — from side to side, top to bottom, corner to corner and front to back. If there is anything you do not like in what you see, try something different, such as another camera angle. This need not take ages, but if you reject unsatisfying pictures before taking them it will prevent the wholly unwelcome surprise, when you see your processed pictures for the first time, of finding things that you did not notice when you pressed the shutter release button.

Try to *fill the frame* whenever possible, whether the subject is static or moving, small or large. A tiny subject lost in an expanse of wasted space is seldom of any interest. Go in close and make it big and bold; the picture will have much more impact. After all, you have to pay for the entire picture area, so you might as well use it.

Avoid bad backgrounds which can accidentally become a part of your main subject or swallow it completely.

If there are prominent lines or shapes behind the subject, either use them to frame it or move it away from them to a different background. Where there is a distracting detail, such as in a patterned wallpaper, use the widest possible aperture so that the pattern will be rendered out of focus. This works better when the subject is close to the camera, or when a lens with a long focal length is used, or both.

Unless the subject occupies roughly a square, or you are using a square film format, consider whether the picture should be *vertical or horizontal*. It is common to see wasted space to either side of a subject, which would have been better framed if the camera had been turned on its side.

In landscape photography *take care with the horizon*: one which cuts the picture precisely in half generates less of a feeling of drama than one which cuts it into unequal halves.

Right: graphic, semi-abstract shapes against different tones of a single colour create a striking image of sunset over the North Sea. Careful choice of viewpoint has given the composition a strong focal centre, breaking the regularity of the guard rail and suggesting depth.

Below: a classically proportioned landscape in which the eye easily follows the road past the trees and to the horizon.

Opposite page, left: featureless and impersonal expanses of wall dominate the image, squeezing into insignificance the human habitations beyond them. The photographer has used his design skill to produce a highly subjective interpretation of life on a modern housing estate.

Opposite page, right: an ordered and almost symmetrical composition in pastel colours. The eye is led down to the water where it is contained by the framework made by the reflections of the trees.

Right: a frame within a frame—often an effective device, here used in a rather tongue-in-cheek manner to draw attention to the diminutive figure at the end of the tunnel.

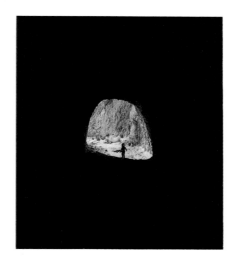

Further suggestions

Composition can further be regarded as the arrangement of shapes, lines and points into a pleasing or appropriate structure.

The eye travels along lines until they are broken, so they can be used to draw the viewer's eye into the subject.

Diagonal lines are dynamic and suggest energy and movement; horizontal and vertical lines are more static. A diagonal composition can often give life to sport and action photography, whereas peaceful landscapes and architectural photographs often benefit from stable verticals and a broad horizontal base.

Symmetrical arrangements are not usually very interesting to look at and fail to stimulate or excite the viewer; the main point of interest (e.g. the eyes of a portrait subject, or the highest of a series of mountain peaks) looks better when placed off-centre in both vertical and horizontal planes.

These are general suggestions only. Other compositional points are raised where relevant in the pages that follow. To develop your pictorial design skills, try analyzing any pictures that you particularly like—paintings as well as photographs, in books, magazines, on advertising hoardings and at exhibitions—and these will stimulate your awareness of composition as an important element of picture making.

Choose a theme or subject

When you have been taking photographs for a while and have accumulated a stack of them in folders or boxes, you may begin to wonder why you took some of them, what you should do with them and whether it is really necessary to take yet more pictures to add to the random collection.

Taking pictures in isolation from each other will almost certainly lead sooner or later to a sense of futility. There is less and less incentive to go out and discover new images for their own sake; interest begins to pall and eventually the camera will spend most of its time gathering dust on the shelf, to be taken down only for the occasional wedding or day at the seaside. The next 56 pages of this book are devoted to describing, with examples, some of the more or less specialized subjects that may stimulate the imagination of the photographer who is looking for something to exercise his skills upon.

Some of the headings are extremely general–the subject of *Holidays*, for example, necessarily encompasses far more in the way of subject matter and camera techniques than does *Flowers* or (it is to be hoped) *Bad weather*. Other categories are much more specialized, e.g. *Interiors*, *Weddings* or

Setting yourself a theme to work to is a way of sustaining your interest in photography even when there is no obvious special event or circumstance (such as a wedding or a family holiday) to arouse it. An enthusiastic photographer will go out to find and develop a subject or theme, rather than just waiting for one to happen to him. You could, for example, choose windows: many effective and imaginative pictures have been taken of subjects such as this. If you keep your eyes open you will discover unexpected possibilities all around.

Above: a stained glass window by Marc Chagall, photographed in a small country church. The techniques of photographing stained glass are described on page 108.

Right: an unusual and evocative view through a train window–not taken by the driver as you might guess, but by a passenger with a watchful eye and an interest in photography.

Sport. There is something here for any photographer who would like to develop his interest in the hobby with whatever degree of involvement.

Each double-page spread in this section is intended to be an introduction to a subject rather than a comprehensive data-sheet on its special requirements. Particularly useful or relevant techniques are suggested where appropriate, with advice on what equipment and materials will generally be found to be most useful. In the case of the more difficult subjects there are hints on how to overcome the likely problems and pitfalls.

The pictures used to illustrate the various themes and subjects have been selected with the problems of the average amateur photographer in mind throughout. These are the kind of photographs that you *can* expect to take. Pictures that could only be obtained by the use of elaborate and costly equipment, or from a vantage point to which a photographer cannot gain access unless he carries a Press pass or similar licence, have not been used. By description and by example, therefore, these pages will be of immense and genuine practical value to all amateur photographers seeking a subject to work on or wishing to increase the scope of their photography.

Top left: a window in a dusty old barn, overgrown with ivy and looking out directly at a broken drainpipe, may not be the most obvious thing to take pictures of; yet it makes a pleasing composition with many subtle grey tones.

Top right: a shuttered window in Venice, conveying some of the charm of the local architecture. Windows do not have to be photographed from the inside to be interesting.

Left: a bleak view of factory windows in an industrial town. At first sight the impression is one of looking up the side of a tall building, but the horizon re-establishes the correct aspect.

Babies and children

Babies and young children are not difficult to photograph well because they are one of the most naturally photogenic subjects of all. The challenge is to produce pictures that are outstanding rather than merely competent.

Take plenty of pictures of your children, especially on birthdays and at other milestones, to be sure of getting a sequence of really good ones. Little children grow up fast, and once missed a birthday never comes back. Informal pictures are easier and often more telling than formal ones: wait until the child or children are absorbed in something—unwrapping presents, painting, having tea—and natural poses will occur together with a variety of facial expressions. You should be able to capture surprise, pleasure and fun, but keep an eye open also for anger and tears.

Photographs can be especially effective if they seem to have been taken from a child's point of view, rather than by an adult looking in at the world of childhood from outside. Perspective is different from down there: adults and their furniture tower up and disappear. Hold the camera at child's-eye level for some of your pictures, and do not worry about cutting off adults at waist level or removing the upper parts of pieces of furniture—it all helps to recreate a

child's unique perspective on life. If you want a more formal type of portrait, rather than dress the child up especially for a camera session wait until he is being dressed up anyway—for a party, say, or for his first day at school. The picture will be less spontaneous, but not necessarily wooden or unnatural.

Do not forget the problem of colour balance if you take pictures indoors by artificial light. If your camera is loaded with daylight reversal film the least problematic solution will probably be to use electronic flash, preferably bounced; this will override the artificial lighting.

The use of colour correction filters (as described on page 54) is less satis-factory as they reduce effective film speed, and unless you are using a fast film—of about 400 ASA—this restric-tion can make it difficult to use a fast enough shutter speed to get the results you want. Children rarely stay still for long enough to please their parents, photographers or not.

For a baby asleep in the pram or a toddler in the cot, the soft light created by bounced flash will give a more pleasing effect than direct flash with its rather aggressive frontal lighting and hard black shadows.

When children are old enough to

Top: one of the easiest ways to take effective photographs of children is to catch them at play. In this picture the rim of the barrel provides a natural frame for the portrait of the child. (It also helped to make sure he did not run away without warning.) The photographer has been careful to focus on the eyes, as depth of field is restricted at close range.

Right: the child on the slide is naturally excited by the interest being shown in him. The colours are simple and bold and the eye is led easily into the subject by careful framing of the shot.

know about cameras and what they are for it may be more difficult to get them to pose naturally. A telephoto lens can be useful here, as it enables the photographer to stay back out of the way and be less obtrusive. A lens of about 135mm with a 35mm single-lens reflex would be a good choice. It will also be useful for photographing older children's team games which, being more organized, require more concentration on the part of the players and hence create some good opportunities for candid shots.

Think of other children too, not just your own: children playing in the streets or walking from school in a crocodile, or looking bored or mischievous while their elders are preoccupied with other matters.

Top left: the children playing in the fountain were unaware of the camera, but the photographer had to time his shot carefully for this well-balanced composition.

Centre left: taken from a low angle, this picture recreates a child's eye view of the world.

Top right: a sensitive study of children absorbed in saying grace. When they get used to seeing a camera around they will lose interest in it, giving you more freedom to select your viewpoint and shoot at exactly the right moment.

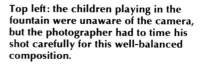

Left: the jaunty angle at which the baby wears his hat belies his serious expression, and the unusual camera viewpoint adds to the humour.

Pets and animals

Pet portraits can lapse into sentimentality unless the photographer
guards against this danger. When
deciding how to approach the subject, therefore, take time to think
about it before picking up the
camera; the sort of kitten pictures
used on chocolate boxes appeal to
some people, but may be entirely
inappropriate for the subject in
question. Try to bring out the
animal's character as if you were
describing it to a total stranger: for
example a cat which has an independent attitude may be more truthfully
portrayed in silhouette, prowling
along the garden wall, than lying on a
rug in front of the fire or playing with
a ball of wool.

Small caged animals such as
hamsters or budgerigars may be
difficult to photograph except through
the bars of their cages. The problem is
minimized if the camera lens is placed
right up to the bars: depth of field
limitations will ensure that they
appear only as a blur if they are not
entirely eliminated. By this method
you can probably get the subject
near to filling the frame as well,
although it is important to focus
accurately.

Show the speed of fast-moving
animals such as horses and dogs by
using the technique known as
panning—following the moving subject
in the viewfinder and keeping the
exposure time quite slow—1/60 to
1/30 second or so—to blur the background. On occasions when an
animal is running towards you at such
speed that you cannot focus in time,
the technique known as prefocusing
may help. Prefocusing is focusing on
a spot where you know the subject
will be passing as it races towards
you; the nearer that point is, the more
critical the timing will be. Press the
shutter a moment before you expect
the animal to get there. Shutter speed
should be fast, because you do not
want motion blur in this kind of
picture.

Garden birds and other animals not
really tame enough to be approached
closely can be attracted in front of the
camera by the lure of food. The
camera must be standing on a firm
support, and is operated from a
distance by a long cable release with
an air bulb at the end. The photographer can then remain sufficiently
concealed from the animals until the
exposure has been made. Exposure
and focus settings must be set with
care for this sort of work. Choose the
largest aperture that is compatible
with depth of field requirements, so
that shutter speed can be as fast as
possible. If there is a lot of sky in the
picture—if for example you have set
your camera up pointing at a bird
table—be careful to meter only the
subject, or you may get a sequence of
silhouettes.

For animal photography a fast film
should be selected; many animals
move fast and unpredictably. A
telephoto lens will often help.

There is more about animal photography of a more ambitious sort in
Wildlife and Zoos on page 124.

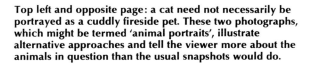

Top left and opposite page: a cat need not necessarily be portrayed as a cuddly fireside pet. These two photographs, which might be termed 'animal portraits', illustrate alternative approaches and tell the viewer more about the animals in question than the usual snapshots would do.

Above, centre: the photographer set his camera up on a tripod and, using a long cable release with an air bulb, waited at a nearby window for the squirrel to be lured in front of the lens by some nuts.

Left: you do not need to photograph the whole animal. This moderately close up view of a pony was taken with a 200mm telephoto lens.

Right: the puppy at play makes a natural sequence, although in this instance it tells a tale that he might not be very proud of. Make a good number of exposures if you want to make a sequence that tells a story, choosing for final presentation the ones that show the key moments.

Fairs, festivals and carnivals

Wherever people get together in public to celebrate and to enjoy themselves there is scope for some exciting photographs to be taken. Apart from the potential of the subject material, these events provide the photographer anxious to improve his visual awareness and camera technique with a useful opportunity to do so. Things happen fast—people group and regroup around different stalls and sights; a parade passes; laughter or quarrels develop, while children run around under the feet of their parents or sit on their shoulders to get a better view. To capture the moments that symbolize the event amid all the formless hubbub you need to think and react fast, because the photographer can only record such happenings and not control them.

Work alone if at all possible. Your eyes need to be scanning the scene, not watching to see what your family or friends are doing. You may also want to duck and weave among the crowds; a lone photographer can do this, but one pulling a family group along will jostle people and cause annoyance.

Take some photographs from a vantage point outside the main centre of gathering, then when you display the photographs you can contrast the distant overall views (of , say, a fairground) with others taken in the thick of the action.

Above: all the gaiety and the riotous colour of the street carnival are captured in this energetic photograph. It was taken by a photographer working on his own and using a medium speed film (Ektachrome 200). A vertical format is often appropriate to such subjects as it can be used to emphasize vitality and movement and give a picture a dynamic feel.

Left: swinging the camera round to follow the subject (panning) creates an impression of speed. The panning technique is more fully described on pages 122-123.

Left: a long shot of the Red Devils taken at an air fair using a moderate telephoto lens. In photography of this sort, take special care not to expose for the sky, which is quite bright and would result in the aeroplanes being underexposed.

Below: a telephoto lens is not only useful for distant shots of subjects such as aeroplanes—at close range it can be used to pick out and magnify details such as the faces of people who are clearly enjoying themselves.

Bottom: specialized fairs provide an opportunity for the enthusiast to have a field day, whether his principal interest is in photography, traction engines or whatever else might be on display.

Assemblies that take place during the hours of dusk and darkness are rich with potential, as lighting effects are likely to be unusual and atmospheric. Using a film of about 400 ASA you will be able to take plenty of pictures without flash (which would give nearby objects a daylight coloration and tend to destroy the atmosphere). Set the camera to its widest aperture and the shutter speed to 1/30 second for most of the exposures, unless you know from experience that you prefer a different effect. Try one or two smaller apertures, and a few at 1/15 second if you can support the camera really firmly.

Effective pictures of fairgrounds can be taken by time exposure, for which a tripod is indispensable. Try 1 second at f/16 with 400 ASA film (f/5.6 with 100 ASA). Experiment with longer exposures if you like, but do not forget that the response of colour emulsions is unpredictable at exposures of longer than 1 second. However even this speed is long enough for bright moving lights to record as streaks of colour.

As you may have limited space to work in, a wide-angle lens can be a valuable asset for crowd shots. At air fairs, and at other festivals where a parade or military band may approach from a distance, good use can be made of telephoto lenses. When you have a telephoto lens fitted, do not concentrate on distant shots to the exclusion of any other: it can be used to isolate details closer by, such as interesting faces in the crowd.

Capturing the spirit of Christmas

There is probably more to photograph indoors at Christmas time than at any other time of year. There will also be additional incentive to think about photography because cameras are so obviously a good Christmas present.

If you intend to buy a camera as a present, make sure that the recipient will be able to use it: either get it in a gift pack containing film and any batteries or flash attachments that may be necessary, or purchase these items separately as part of the gift, budget permitting. It is disappointing to have to wait until the shops open before a new camera can be used.

For experienced photographers the Christmas and New Year period is a fertile time. Amid the parties, reunions and colourful rituals goodwill abounds and the presence of cameras will surprise nobody. This is the time to take candid portraits—when people are relaxed and happy and their behaviour is natural.

Lighting can be a problem in the gloom of winter in the northern hemisphere. Use tungsten film for pictures taken by the light of ordinary domestic bulbs. Candles and decorative Christmas tree lights are too dim for normal photography, but will show as brightly colourful points when the

Above: the Christmas decorations in Regent Street, London. When strings of coloured bulbs are used to form a massed display there is a good chance of getting a fair result with most cameras, even non-adjustable models; but for spectacular shots like this one in situations where metering is almost impossible it is always wise to take two or three pictures at different exposures, to be sure of getting at least one really good one. But do not be tempted to use flash— it will make no difference at all in situations like this.

Right: flash is used here to good effect. Its light is strong enough to override most artificial sources, so ordinary daylight-type films can successfully be used.

Left: be ready with a camera when children start helping to pillage the Christmas tree; they will be far too busy and excited to worry about what you are doing. The same applies to the ritual of unwrapping the presents: a sequence such as that at the bottom of this page, registering the transition of the boy's facial expression from excited anticipation to delight, will never be more easily recorded than it is in these circumstances.

Below: an unpretentious snapshot which has captured the spontaneous atmosphere of Christmas Day festivities. More or less any camera can be used to take photographs of subjects lit by direct sun, even indoors, although the final result might be rather contrasty.

main light is from another source, so do not worry about their colour quality. If you are uncertain about the lighting, try to include a background that unmistakably belongs to Christmas—the tree with glass baubles and fairy lights, paper chains, holly with berries, candles, crackers—any of these will establish an environment for the main subject and explain whatever colour balance may appear in photographs.

Since all the tinsel and baubles of Christmas are artificial anyway there is no harm in adding to the impression by the use of special effects filters: starbursts and prisms are obvious examples, but most filters can be used to better effect now than at most other times.

It is perhaps at Christmas that instant picture photography really comes into its own. Not only do instant cameras make ideal gifts, they are also compatible with the convivial and spontaneous atmosphere of the occasion. Try to maintain the usual standards as regards composition, backgrounds and so on, but do not let such considerations spoil the fun.

Holidays — strange lands and people

Travelling away from home presents a photographer with challenges and opportunities. Perhaps the greatest challenge is to avoid the obvious—to come home with pictures of genuine originality, not just picture-postcard views (although these also play their part). The advice is easier to give than to follow.

If you do not travel more than once or twice a year, and especially if you visit different places rather than making an annual pilgrimage to the same inevitable resort, a photographic record of your journeys will keep them fresh in your mind long after they would otherwise have vanished in the mists of time. So pack plenty of film, and do not be hampered in using it—consider it part of the holiday expenses rather than a hobbyist's luxury. Photograph the people as well as the places, the interiors of buildings as well as the exteriors, the unknown sights as well

Below: scenes containing areas of deep blue water often have strong, saturated colours which can benefit from slight underexposure—perhaps half to one stop under the metered setting. Here it has also helped to preserve detail in the pale-coloured boats, which could easily become thin and washed out.

Above: when taking a photograph of a majestic view remember that large expanses of bright sky can influence a built-in exposure meter in such a way that detail will be lost in the landscape. Open up by a stop or two, according to how much of the picture the sky occupies and how bright it is.

as the famous ones, the ugly as well as the beautiful. Try to capture the essence of the area you are visiting. Have patience; afterwards you will always be thankful that you did. Many potentially good photographs have been missed in the past for want of stopping the car.

For many people holidays are essentially family events. By all means include members of the family in plenty of your pictures—but not all of them. When you want to picture a person together with a well-known monument, pay careful attention to perspective: do not pose people so that they are dwarfed by the building, for probably either the people will come out too small to be recognizable, or the building too large, vanishing off the edges of the frame. Move the person or people away from the monument until both subjects are identifiable, yet balanced. Make sure that depth of field is adequate to take in both; use a wide-angle lens if you possess one, and be sure not to waste any of the picture area. If this is impossible take two photographs and display them together: one showing the monument, the other showing the person with a well-chosen detail to represent the setting. This will be clear enough if thoughtfully done.

Think back to your choice of destination: photograph the things that originally attracted you to the area, and the other things you are bound to find when you get there.

Use tact when photographing people in foreign countries. Nobody likes the feeling of being subjected to scrutinizing stares and prying lenses, and in some circumstances a photographer can get into trouble for photographing things the authorities or local inhabitants disapprove of. If in doubt, ask permission. In other circumstances, of course, people expect to be photographed: at amusement parks and fairs, on the beach or sitting at pavement cafés the sight of a camera will not offend the majority; nevertheless, always be considerate of others.

When holidaying in sunny climates take care that you do not allow a bright sky to influence your exposure meter, causing underexposure of the main subject.

Presentation of holiday pictures is often best done in sequence—not a story with a punch line, that is, more a travelogue. Start at the very beginning with pictures of your departure, if you can, followed by the journey, however made; photograph signposts and place names as well as curiosities, and finish with some homeward-bound shots. Photographers who specialize in a particular subject (e.g. architecture) will no doubt pursue their interest, which

may after all be the principal reason for their choice of holiday, but do not neglect the more informal side of photography.

Take as much equipment as you can carry, making sure before you go that it is all in working order, and a book such as this one to consult when particular problems arise.

Top: the beach offers plenty of opportunities to photograph people— there is always something happening. Pictures of friends and relations in high spirits and jumping around help to liven up albums of holiday snaps; a gallery of sunbathers and drink- sippers will look dull and uneventful.

Above, centre: a lively photograph which has captured the bustle and local colour of a holiday resort in Gran Canaria. If you choose your exposure settings in advance you can quickly shoot this kind of scene before the people in it become conscious of the camera.

Left: although it is obviously a good idea to keep your camera handy for moments such as this, do not leave photographic equipment hanging around unprotected on the beach. Apart from the risk of having it stolen the combined effects of sand, salt spray and the heat of the sun can damage film and shorten the working life of camera mechanisms. At the very least it should be kept in a bag wrapped in a towel—preferably a white one— or something similar.

The sun and sunsets

The main problem with photographs in which the sun appears is that of accurately metering the light. This will not concern the user of a non-adjustable camera who, contrary to what many people believe, can often take spectacularly successful pictures of the setting sun.

When it sits high in a cloudless sky the sun is, to a photographer, simply the strongest light source of all. He will not need to think of the orb itself as an element of his composition – only in terms of the quality and direction of the light it delivers (except in the case of the astronomical photographer taking pictures of solar phenomena such as sunspots or an eclipse). But in the hours following sunrise and preceding sunset it is sometimes desirable to include the sun in pictures.

The metering problem arises because being such an intensely bright source the sun will upset any built-in exposure system, including a spot meter, if it is within the image area. The meter will read the *whole* scene as being bright, and will compensate by giving a readout that is considerably under what it should be. You may still get a picture – a very effective one, even – but it will be a picture that happened to you, and not one that you, the photographer, conceived and made. A skilful photo-grapher can identify situations like this and choose what effect he wants – which may or may not be the same as the effect the meter wants.

Using an incident light meter (see page 146) is the best way to get round this problem; but the majority of amateur photographers rely on built-in systems. If you have auto-matic exposure control without manual override you have no choice (unless you can alter the film speed setting), but try anyway, especially if the sun is low on the horizon or actually setting. If you do not have automatic exposure control, or can override it, take a reading with the camera facing at right-angles to the

Above: a 400mm telephoto lens has magnified the sun to eight times the size at which you would normally expect to see it in a 35mm photograph.

Right: when low on the horizon, the sun radiates a reddish light that, although not as bright as earlier in the day, is still powerful and contrasty. The coastline has been reduced to dense black shapes.

direction of the sun. Then over or under expose or abide by the meter reading as your creative instincts dictate.

If this suggests it is difficult to take a good sunset it is misleading; on the contrary, any photograph taken into the setting sun is likely to be dramatic and powerful. It is more difficult if you wish to retain foreground detail, but taking several shots at different exposures (bracketing) should ensure

that there will be at least one good one.

The composition will often create itself, too. As the sun sets the light changes very rapidly, so do not wait to get a better viewpoint. If there is nothing special about it—a pylon silhouetted in the foreground, a surrealistic cloud formation—it is unlikely to have caught your attention in the first place. The colour of the light is vivid red at that time of day.

The impact of a sunset photo depends on this coloration, so do not attempt to correct it with filters.

Silhouettes are a case of extra high contrast and occur when the photographer, by design or by accident, allows a brilliant background to influence exposure so that objects in the foreground drop into dense black, with no detail visible. This effect may be difficult to avoid in sunset scenes but fortunately it often improves them.

Top left: a starburst filter has been used to make the sun the dominant element of this surrealistic composition.

Above: part of the image has been completely burnt out by the strong sunlight, and backlighting makes the apple blossom glow against the dark background.

Top right: when the setting sun moves behind clouds it will often throw out curtains or fans of light. Meter for the sky if you want to photograph this effect.

Above: the sea is often calm at sunset and makes an ideal setting for serene and peaceful images.

Landscape — portraying the earth's surface

This is one of the great themes of photography, and one which almost everyone broaches at one time or another. A good landscape can be much more than just a pictorial record of some nice scenery: it is a kind of portrait on a large scale of a section of the earth's surface, and may take in anything that rests on it, not just fields and trees.

First, remember to think of the finished picture when you look through the viewfinder. The view from a high building or mountain road may be awe-inspiring, but the camera can only show a relatively small rectangle to represent the whole. The photographer's job is to make sure that that rectangle is interesting in itself, not simply as part of something else. So ignore the totality of the scene and look only at what the viewfinder shows.

The sky is often boring in landscape photographs but it can be improved if there is any cloud in it by the use of filters. With black and white film use a yellow, orange or red filter to darken the blue sky so that the clouds stand out. A polarizing filter will do the same with both colour and black and white films (see pages 64-67 for a fuller explanation). An alternative with colour film is to use a graduated blue filter to intensify the blue at the top of the picture.

Good composition is vital to a successful landscape photograph. It is essentially a static subject, so there is no action or event to provide the main centre of interest, there is only scale and perspective, the balance of shapes and the interplay of light and shade. These elements need not all come together at once.

Make use of scale and perspective by including a foreground such as buildings, plants or trees, or other objects of known size—people if you like—to give depth to the picture. A landscape photograph in which everything is in the far distance is likely to look flat and dull. Also make use of any elements in the scenery that can lead the eye to the strong point of the picture: roads, fences, lines of trees, anything linear can be used. Bold shapes are often enough in themselves to make a striking photograph, but they need to be well balanced: the dominant shape should not be placed in the centre of the picture, but to one side. Similarly the horizon is weak if it cuts the picture into equal halves; point the camera up or down to make either the sky or the land dominate the image. A picture which is three-quarters sky is expansive and usually placid; one in which there is little or no sky at the top tends to enhance the energetic, even disquieting qualities of the landscape.

For most landscape work the sun is the only light source. Frontal or top lighting flattens contours, and for this reason it is usually better to avoid photographing in the middle of the day. When sunlight is sloping in at an angle it creates more interesting patterns of light and shadow, emphasizing texture and any irregularity of the terrain.

Two industrial landscapes, each of which is successful in a different way. The upper picture has a rosy glow and silhouette effect that make an almost romantic impression, despite the unpleasant connotations of the subject. The lower one is almost completely devoid of colour: the motionless cranes mirrored in the glassy-calm surface of the water have a tranquil air.

Take care not to allow a bright sky to influence a built-in exposure meter: this can result in underexposure of the land. Work out the correct exposure by tilting the camera down so that sky is excluded from the metered area.

The landscape is a considered work, one over which the photographer has taken as much time as necessary to select his viewpoint, exposure and materials. A wide-angle lens, taking in a broader sweep of the vista both horizontally and vertically, is a great asset and will probably be used more than any other, but lenses of all focal lengths have their place and each can capture the essence of a place in a different way. A good tripod should also be available for the longer exposures needed at dusk and in other poor light situations and to maximize depth of field. The scope of black and white photography will be considerably increased by a set of filters as described on pages 64-65.

When looking for landscape subjects, do not forget urban and industrial areas as well as the more usual countryside ones. Making a

good photograph out of unpromising subject material is more satisfying to the enthusiast than simply snapping away at the local beauty spot, which anyone can do.

Top: trees can be portrayed as elements in a wider landscape (left), or standing alone in monolithic grandeur (right).

Above, centre: a mellow landscape suffused with the warm light of an autumn morning. The sun, sloping in from iow down in the sky, throws into relief the gentle undulations of the land.

Right: a well-composed photograph taken in the Tyrolean Alps.

Night photography

Anything that can be seen at night (or any other time) can be photographed; also the night can make a subject in itself, and can be simulated by fairly simple means.

If your camera does not offer adjustable shutter speeds you will not be able to take consistently well-exposed photographs at night, although using 400 ASA film it is still possible to take satisfactory shots of reasonably bright subjects such as neon signs, which are their own light source. If you enjoy experimenting, try anyway—you may be pleasantly surprised; but also be prepared for a few disappointments unless there is a really good concentration of light in every shot.

For a serious attempt at night-time photography a tripod is an essential accessory, together with a lockable cable release. Armed with these and a fast film you can turn night into day, although not for action shots. Using 400 ASA film you should be able to take pictures by street lighting alone with an exposure of about 1/2 second at f/16 (for maximum depth of field) or 1/30 second at f/4 if you do not have a tripod. However there are no hard-and-fast rules because the distribution and brightness of street lighting can vary. The safest bet is to bracket the exposures—to take additional pictures at one stop more and one stop less than the estimated exposure—and choose the best of the

Above right: although orange is supposedly a 'warm' colour, there is little warmth in this desolate scene. The anonymity of the motorway architecture at night combines with the unwelcoming coldness and damp of the foggy air to convey a sense of alienation.

Right: the town of Berga in northern Spain—a twenty-minute exposure from a hillside above the town, with the camera mounted on a tripod. The greenish coloration of the light is caused by the failure of the layers of colour emulsion to react at a constant rate when exposures of longer than about 1 second are made.

three; better still, if it is an important subject and you want to be sure of getting one good photograph, vary the estimated exposure by one and two stops each way—then you will have five to choose from.

Films can be push-processed to increase their effective speed. This is not difficult if you do your own processing, but if you go to a dealer check that the service is available before you expose the film. You will probably be able to get a 400 ASA film uprated to 800 ASA for a small additional charge. This means you simply set the film speed to 800 ASA on a camera with built-in exposure meter.

If the shutter is left open for a longish period any moving lights will record as lines of colour, which is how the spectacular ribbon-like shots of car head and tail lights are achieved. Set the aperture to f/8 or f/11 and leave the camera on a tripod with the shutter locked on the B setting until you judge that enough cars have passed. The same principle can be used to record the stars

wheeling around in the night sky, but the stars are much fainter than car lights, so open the camera lens to its widest aperture and leave the shutter open for a good ten minutes, or an hour if you can. A wide-angle lens takes in a broader sweep of the sky than a standard lens.

Creating night artificially can be done by means of filters: a blue filter

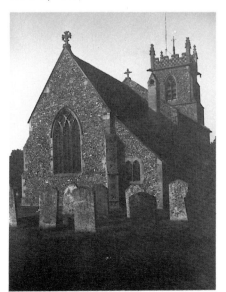

with colour film and a red one with black and white. The blue filter will darken everything and create an artificial moonlight effect with colour films; the red filter will blacken the sky in black and white photography—a remarkable effect. Another way is to underexpose the picture with either type of film, but this is really only effective in very contrasty scenes.

Top left: Fifth Avenue, New York, taken with a single-lens reflex camera hand held at a shutter speed of 1/15 second. You can safely use daylight-type film for street scenes at night: if this shot had been taken on film balanced for tungsten lighting the colours would have been more neutral, but not necessarily better.

Top right: it is possible to take good colour photographs by moonlight, especially if the moon is full or nearly full. Exposure was about one minute—just long enough for the movement of the moon to show.

Left: a thirteen-minute exposure by moonlight. Notice the cold clarity of the moon's light in the dust-free night air.

The seasons in town and countryside

This is not really a special category of photography, but it is a good example of a theme which any keen photographer can adopt and develop to his own personal style. It can be undertaken with any equipment from the most primitive to the most sophisticated, anywhere and at any time. Having a permanent project of this kind is a good incentive to keep your camera ready throughout the year (if any incentive is needed); at the same time it can supply a considerable challenge to your creativity and originality if you set out to avoid the clichés. It can also provide a suitable subject for any specific technique that you may want to practice. For example, if you want to master the business of when and how to override the automatic exposure facility your camera offers, you can do this knowing that the successful pictures will go into a growing portfolio of seasonal pictures and not merely clutter the shelves as an interesting technical exercise. Another benefit is that it will make an excellent exercise in presentation.

The seasons are mostly associated with nature and the countryside because this is where the greatest changes take place. But the intrinsic nostalgia value of the subject can also be exploited in towns to at least as good effect, and the images, although scarcely less evocative, will almost certainly be less obvious. Towns respond in subtle ways to the cycle of the seasons: you will see it in the ways people dress, in their attitude to their environment, in the ways in which commercial centres present themselves to the public. The changeability of the weather manifests itself with more obvious signs: rain, snow and fog in the streets as opposed to warm sunshine. Watch for the effects of sudden change such as unexpected showers, gusts of wind etc. To isolate the moment that characterizes a season and to fix it on photographic film is no easy achievement.

Consider whether to combine your pictures as a narrative or as a record of inexorable cyclical change, starting

and finishing at the same point. Alternatively, contrast views of the same subject in different conditions: a well-frequented café, say, spilling out on to the pavements and brimming with life in the summer sun, then with tables and chairs deserted in the rain, then again closed against the elements in winter but still announcing itself good-humouredly to the world.

Agriculture is a natural subject as it is based entirely on the annual cycle of growth and decay, and with farmers working on the land there is always something to photograph.

Taken on successive days, this pair of photographs demonstrates the remarkable swiftness with which the transition from one season to the next can take place. Within the space of less than twenty-four hours the deep, sunlit hues of late autumn have given way to the bleak monochromatic tones of winter. No given set of seasonal conditions can be guaranteed to last for long – autumn may return as quickly as winter appeared to set in – so a vigilant photographer will be out in all weathers trying to capture the essence of the time.

90

Top left and centre: contrasting images of winter. Out in the country, frost on the twigs always makes an interesting pattern. In the photograph of New York the real subject is the striking contrast between the strong curves of the broken ice and the rigid verticals of the buildings beyond.

Top right: autumn colours are especially evocative in fine weather. The photographer has chosen a low camera angle to make the few remaining withered leaves stand out against the pale blue of the sky.

Centre: one image of summer. The combine harvester has a curious air of loneliness about it, caused by the apparent featurelessness of the flat land and the lack of cloud in the large expanse of sky.

An apple orchard in spring is an uplifting sight, but beware of allowing photographs of such spectacles to degenerate into mere sentimentality. The luxuriant blossoms are held together in this picture by the suggestion of the tree trunk, behind them and out of focus.

Bad weather — it pays to brave the elements

The meteorological conditions we habitually lump together as 'bad weather' are not equally nasty for everyone. Many bad weather phenomena, far from depriving a photographer of subject matter, actually provide him with it, although sportsmen and farmers may curse profoundly when wind and rain strike. It takes enthusiasm to go out with a camera in inclement weather, but the rewards are there.

Rain alters the appearance of the landscape, muting colours and softening outlines. If you take pictures showing this they will be unusual because relatively few people are prepared to do it, and sometimes the effect is very beautiful. Following a shower there may be a period of translucence and clarity because the dust has been rained out of the atmosphere, and here again the enterprising photographer can exploit the conditions. You will need enough shelter to protect the lens in rainy conditions, but an umbrella—preferably carried by someone else—should

be enough if the rain is not driven by wind; and a skylight or ultraviolet filter will also be useful.

Wet city streets at night reflect car and traffic lights, the neon signs and the street lamps, and these add interest to night-time pictures by effectively doubling the number of light sources you can include in the picture.

In a strong wind, slender trees and branches sway while grass and foliage bend and shake: use a slow shutter speed with the camera mounted on a tripod to capture some of this restless energy. With a slow film (100 ASA or less) you should be able to reduce the shutter speed to around 1/15 second or less at f/16 in overcast conditions, and this will allow windswept plants to blur without completely losing their identity.

To photograph a rainbow, take a meter reading and underexpose by one stop; if you are prepared to bracket exposures, try at 1, 1½ and 2 stops below the meter reading. A rainbow is effectively a light source,

and a degree of underexposure will enhance colour saturation within it; but the rest of the picture will of course be correspondingly darker.

Mist and fog, like the setting sun, can make effective photographs even when exposure is technically incorrect, although not always. City streets, railway stations and similar lamplit subjects take on almost Victorian air, while out in the country trees shrouded in early morning mist

Below left: a chill and misty morning in an unpromising environment might dampen the enthusiasm of many photographers, but every place has its own atmosphere and there are invariably some fine compositions to be discovered by those who take the trouble to look.

Below: torrential rain has flooded the marquee while wedding preparations were in full swing, causing a flurry of activity. In temperate climates rain is rarely heavy enough to show up at all on film; here, at a shutter speed of 1/30 second, it has been recorded as a distinctly visible curtain of water.

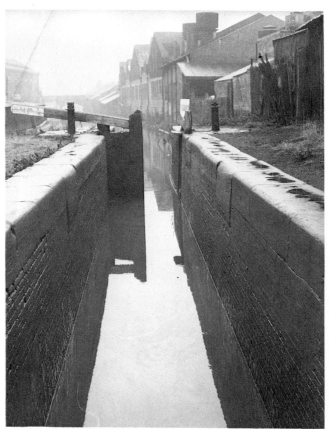

become sometimes peaceful, sometimes ghostly. Again the advice is to bracket your exposures.

Make use of filters in black and white photography to emphasize a cloudy sky. For a stormy effect a red filter is best.

Unless you are going for a motion-blur effect as described above it is best to use a fast film in dull or changeable weather. Light levels vary, but are seldom very bright.

Below: it is not always easy to envisage the results you will get in extreme weather conditions, so it pays to take two or three at different exposures. In foul weather a slightly underexposed picture can help to exaggerate the feeling of gloom.

Bottom: high winds and the failing light of an overcast evening were the environmental factors that made this delicate colour composition possible. The picture was taken on fairly slow film (64 ASA) at a shutter speed of 1/2 second with the camera mounted on a tripod. The ash tree in the foreground has lost detail throughout.

Above: the blackish-purple light of heavy rain clouds is barely relieved by the pink of the setting sun.

Bottom right: a forlorn landscape, completely waterlogged after heavy rain and with every sign in the sky that there is more to come.

Below: Lords cricket ground during the Centenary Test, England versus Australia, in August 1980. Rain stopped play with Australia at 278-4 in their first innings. A few bright umbrellas remained to make this melancholy picture.

Water, both still and flowing

As a photographic subject, water is like children in that it has people reaching for their cameras almost before they are aware of what they are doing. Water has a quality that attracts people to it as if by magnetism: garden planners are familiar with this pattern of behaviour and often make a fountain or cascade the focal point of a garden design, knowing that visitors will inevitably turn their footsteps towards it like pilgrims flocking to a shrine.

It is not, therefore, a question of whether to photograph water, but of when and how to photograph it. When calm it will reflect the scenery beyond with mirror-like fidelity, which is perfect for compositions of serene symmetry. However this in itself is not always enough: the lighting should still be angled so that there is modelling in the landscape, and other compositional elements need not be neglected just because they appear doubled.

When buildings stand near water it is an interesting variation on a theme to photograph only the reflection and exclude the building itself; this is particularly true if the surface of the water is rippled rather than glassy-calm. Do not do this in all cases, because the impression would become jaded and monotonous. If you go down close to the water to photograph a reflection remember to focus on the reflected image and not on the surface of the water. Automatic focusing systems can be confused in these circumstances, so if your automatic focusing camera offers the facility to do so, lock the focus on the actual subject before framing its reflection in the water.

Reflected glare can detract from the appearance of water and interfere with built-in metering systems. Fit a polarizing filter to reduce the effect. Another filter that may be used to advantage—sparingly—is the starburst, which will catch the flickering highlights and turn them into bright pointed stars.

There are two different approaches to flowing water in fountains, streams

94

Above: a single stop can make a surprising amount of difference to the degree of movement recorded in fast-flowing water. The upper picture was taken at 1/500 second, the lower one at 1/125.

Above right: if the sea is fairly calm take your camera right out to where the action is. Do not do this in rough conditions as salt water can damage photographic equipment.

and cascades. The first is to use a fast shutter speed to freeze the motion, so that every droplet is caught suspended in the air and little jets and splashes take on the appearance of distorted icicles. The second is to use a slow speed, which gives the water a smoother, more flowing appearance. This approach is more impressionistic and, on balance, more appropriate to

the majority of water subjects. However the choice is yours, as long as your camera has adjustable shutter speeds, and you have a tripod for the slow exposure. To freeze the motion use the fastest speed the conditions will allow—preferably 1/500-1/1000 second; to blur it use the slowest—1/30 second if you have no tripod, but preferably slower.

Opposite page, top: an impression of tremendous depth is achieved by putting the emphasis on the reflection of the trees rather than on the trees themselves. Exclude the sun from the viewfinder area when metering this type of subject.

Opposite page, bottom: direct sun on the water makes a sparkling background for this impressionistic but graphic nature study.

Right: fresh water from a tufa spring pouring on to rocks on the beach. Shutter speed was 1/15 second, and the camera was mounted on a tripod.

The sea and seascapes

The sea with its many faces and many moods has been the subject of pictures for as long as man has been able to make them. Even the most basic camera can be used to produce beautiful sea pictures, so that the portrayal of this protean world is now within reach of every photographer, whether beginner or expert.

The sea on its own has to be very dramatic or it lacks interest. When it is calm, try to include the sun or moon in the picture, with a sparkling light path reflected in the water. This creates an impression of depth and gives the picture a focal point. Include some foreground shapes in the scene, or better still some kind of ship,

Below: the low angle of the light on a winter afternoon, casting the shade of coastal hills on to the surf, has created a range of strong blue hues which can be made even more intense by slight underexposure.

Bottom: the use of a 400mm lens has piled up the cliffs in this seascape taken in Cornwall. Including a human figure or two lends a sense of scale to rugged scenery.

because if there is no object of identifiable size perspective is lost; when the great sweep of the horizon is condensed into a small rectangle the vastness of the ocean is reduced to insignificance and its energy dissipated.

Ships and boats make a good subject in their own right, not only as elements in composition. To photograph boats try to go out in one yourself and get near enough to the action to take pictures without intruding (especially if there is a race on). In such circumstances, always use an ultraviolet filter to protect the lens from spray as well as to filter out some of the distance haze. A lens hood is also a useful accessory. If you cannot put to sea, a telephoto lens may enable you to take photographs of boats, water-skiers and so on without wasting a great proportion of the picture on featureless expanses of sea.

There are ways of using the sea in photography other than merely presenting it as a watery version of a landscape. It is appropriate to take

pictures of maritime towns from out at sea, perhaps from an approaching ferry. This can be done at night as well as during the day, an especially favourable time being a few minutes after sunset, when there is still some light in the sky.

Details of marine flora and fauna are not difficult to photograph and are an interesting variation on the main theme. In tidal seas rock pools are often to be found teeming with life at low tide, while seaweeds, pebbles, flotsam and jetsam are suitable subjects for more abstract photography. In tideless seas such as the Mediterranean there is a profusion of colourful growth at the water line.

Below: stormy conditions often provide dramatic lighting for sea pictures, while pointing the camera out over the stern of a power boat has contributed an impression of surging energy.

Bottom: an interesting foreground sets the scene for this maritime composition and helps to frame the shot expensively, as is appropriate to the subject.

An almost abstract view of
the sea, and one which in
spite of—or perhaps
because of—its extreme
simplicity effectively
portrays the vastness and
energy of the oceans. The
lighting gives the surface
of the water a physical
quality of wetness so
tangible that we can almost
hear the waves and smell the
salt in the air. The effect
is compounded by the stormy
darkness of the sky, against
which the waves stand out in
vivid relief as they roll
in towards the shore.
Technically, avoid being
misled by a built-in exposure
meter when photographing
choppy water against the
light—it is all too easy
to underexpose.

Below: not a seascape—
there is after all no water
in the picture—but there
is no mistaking the maritime
flavour of this photograph
of the lobster pots in a
Cornish fishing village.

For many of these subjects the closest
focusing distance of a 35mm camera
will be adequate; but for more
detailed work the techniques and
equipment of close-up or macro-
photography (see pages 60-61) should
be studied.

Finally, the sea is one of the few
subjects that may sometimes be
improved by the use of coloured
filters together with colour film. Since
its colour is derived from the sky they
will both be similar in hue; sometimes
they show an insipid milky-whiteness
which can be strengthened by the use
of a filter of a suitable colour, such as
orange or blue. But such effects are
only rarely an improvement and
should be treated with caution.

Plants and flowers

When photographing flowers decide first of all whether to depict them singly or as part of a massed display. (You can of course do both and display the pictures together.)

To photograph a single specimen choose a viewpoint that emphasizes any peculiarities or distinctive growth characteristics of the plant: the best approach is not always to go for a close-up of the open flower, particularly if your interest is in its botanical significance rather than purely ornamental qualities. A tall plant can either be photographed against the sky, or from above against the background of other plants in its environment. All but the shortest plants can be pictured 'in profile'. When photographing plants against the sky make sure that you do not expose for the background unless you want them to appear as silhouettes—which is what tends to happen with automatic exposure control. Preferably take an incident light reading with a hand-held exposure meter; otherwise measure the exposure from plants only by excluding the sky while the reading is taken.

If you want to isolate a specimen plant from its background you can rig up some bulky object to cast shade behind it, leaving the subject in the sun; if this is impossible (for example, if it is not a sunny day) an alternative is to put an artificial background behind it. A large piece of card is ideal provided it is a suitably neutral hue—grey or black would make both flowers and foliage stand out well.

A cultivated flower treated in this way should be a faultless specimen, although these can be hard to find. Blemishes are more acceptable in wild flowers, within reason, but perfect examples are better if they can be found. Remember also that flowering plants do not actually have to be in flower to be interesting: some have unusual buds, others curious seed-heads, while others still retain fine structural detail long after the green parts have withered. Once you have mastered the techniques of close-up photography these will bring a further dimension to your flower photography.

Massed wild flowers can be a

The background here is a piece of grey card which the photographer was carrying with him for the purpose. Arrange the shot so that light falls directly on to the flower you are photographing, but not on to the artificial background. Also, it is essential not to expose for the background, so meter the scene before you put the card in place.

When photographing an individual bloom one way to isolate it from other flowers is to move in as close as your camera will focus—often about 40cm (15in) or so with 35mm cameras—and use a wide aperture. Depth of field will be so restricted that your specimen flower is almost sure to stand out sharply.

problem to photograph in that the heads are mostly very small and unless there is a really thick drift of them they tend to recede into their background. This is worst of all with blue flowers and least troublesome with red and yellow ones. Approach the flowers as closely as you can and get a few good and large in the foreground.

Cultivated flowers in a formal setting are not difficult: let the composition of your photograph reflect the geometric concerns of the gardener. An informal garden can be treated like a wild setting, although it should be easier as the individual blooms will be more prominent and less likely to hide their heads.

Visually the most effective kind of lighting for plants is backlighting from the sun. For a scientific approach flash is more controllable, whether as sole source or as fill-in.

One final word of warning: do not pick or trim wild plants or dig them up, or clear a space round them. Photograph them as you find them in their natural environment, and leave them the same way. Some are rare or in danger of extinction and may be protected by law.

Above: colour is so much a part of the plant world that the treatment of flowers in black and white is seldom effective. This massed display, lit by direct sun and photographed with a wide-angle lens, nevertheless achieves considerable impact.

Left: scarlet flax blowing in the wind, photographed by time exposure with the camera mounted on a tripod. Even slow films are often too fast to permit slow shutter speeds unless the light is exceptionally poor, so if you want to create this sort of effect you should equip yourself with one or more neutral density filters. These reduce the overall intensity of the light without altering its colour or other qualities.

The centre of an ornamental cabbage, photographed from close up and with a small aperture to maximise depth of field. The most beautiful flowers are not the only ones to make good photographs.

Lightning and fireworks

These two subjects are treated together because both require a similar approach and the same equipment. For both it is essential to have a camera with a B shutter speed setting, a lockable cable release and a tripod. Standard or wide-angle lenses will be the most useful.

Lightning is the more difficult to photograph because it is impossible to predict with certainty in which direction it will be seen, and several attempts may be necessary. Fix the camera to the tripod and point it in the direction of any lightning flashes that have been seen. Set the aperture at f/11 using film of 400 ASA (f/5.6 with film of 100 ASA, etc.) and focus on infinity. Open the shutter and lock it, then wait for more flashes. Close the shutter after a single brilliant flash, or after two, three or four lesser ones.

During a thunderstorm you will usually need shelter for this operation, although your chances of success are greater if it is not pouring with rain at the same time. Photographs of lightning can be taken from indoors with the windows open or closed, depending on the conditions; however all interior lights should be switched off to prevent reflected light entering the lens and fogging the film during the long exposures, and of course there has to be a window facing in the direction of the storm. If there is a low-level aura of light from a nearby town (or if you are actually in a town) do not expose for more than a minute or two before giving up the frame and winding on for another attempt. Lightning shots are most successful when taken looking out over water.

Fireworks are easier, although there can still be problems, the first of which is to find a suitable position to set up your equipment. At the major displays this may be exceptionally difficult, but one of the benefits of using time exposure is that a small display can be made to look like a national celebration if a number of individual fireworks are recorded on the same piece of film.

If it is impossible to get close to the centre of the action, retreat to a position where an interesting skyline can be chosen to make a foreground silhouette. Set the camera as for lightning, then make exposures of varying length according to the nature of the display. For example, a great finishing tableau can be treated like an ordinary night time shot (try 1/60

Above: a single catherine wheel, at an exposure of a second or so, makes a spectacular picture. You need a tripod and a cable release for this type of picture, but nothing more elaborate is necessary; certainly you do not have to attend a major fireworks display to get successful photographs.

Right: lightning photographed during a summer storm. As it is impossible to forecast exactly when and where a strike will occur, lengthy exposures are often required. For these you need a camera mounted on a tripod, and a lockable cable release. It is also essential to find a position well away from street and town lights.

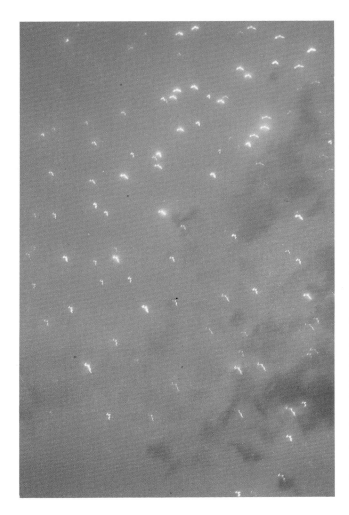

second at f/2.8 with 400 ASA film, but bracket the exposures as a precaution). But if the fireworks are set off one or two at a time it is better to keep the shutter open until several have been recorded.

Firework displays offer an opportunity for experiment. Being artificial in any case they lend themselves to artificial treatment: try out-of-focus effects (some on their own and some mixed with correctly focused bursts);

break the continuous lines by 'chopping' in front of the lens with your hand; use panning techniques, prism and other special effects filters—try anything that comes into your head.

Top left: fireworks can be photographed with a hand-held camera, although you will not get long streamers of coloured light. Here the smoke of previous bursts has been lit up by the pink flares. Shutter speed was 1/30 second at f/5.6.

Top right: another hand-held exposure, this time of the finishing tableau at a major celebration. There is enough light to make a satisfactory exposure on account of the sheer number of explosions taking place simultaneously.

Left: a 135mm telephoto lens was used at f/8 to photograph lightning, again during a summer storm. Note how nearby flashes burn out.

The street life of towns and cities

Urban developments are less often the subject of amateur landscape photography than are rustic scenes, town pictures being more often simple records taken by tourists of the places they have visited. But there is more to the world's major cities than the usual round of towers, churches, statues and parks; and the life of a nation can be represented by the inhabitants of small towns and hamlets as well as those of sprawling conurbations.

The street life of great cities never becomes stale as a photographic subject, as there is always something happening. Photographs which integrate the people and the architecture can be hard to take, yet they are likely to capture the true spirit of a town or city more surely than either in isolation. Observe an area carefully and absorb its atmosphere as you walk around it among the people: decide what sort of people typify the district,

and portray them in their environment. If tourists outnumber the indigenous population, photograph the tourists—their clothes, cameras, dark glasses and purposeless indifference or their excitement; in an industrial district it may be factory workers who give the place its character, while the business and residential quarters of the city each have their own flavour and their peaks and troughs of activity at different times of day.

Smaller towns may offer less variety, but are not often totally devoid of character. Perhaps life moves at a more sedate pace, and your photographs can show this: local people gossiping in the square or on street corners. If you find an area which looks promising but which lacks human interest you could set up the camera and wait until people move into the picture, which they will do sooner or later. Then there are places

which are busy at predictable times— the station when a train arrives, the school when lessons finish, and so on.

Isolated hamlets and village communities range from the too pretty to the very dull. It is no problem to photograph picture-postcard villages, but in a foreign country various details such as architecture and dress will look different and strange and these details can be worth recording on film.

Any camera can be used for photographing community life, and in many ways the less you carry the more likely you are to be able to react quickly to events. Many 35mm photographers consider a wide-angle lens of about 35mm to be ideal in these circumstances, the 50mm lens taking in too narrow an angle of view. Since this is the lens fitted to many 110 pocket and 35mm compact cameras in any case they are equal to most situations in this context.

A steel band makes an exuberant contrast with the old church in front of which they have elected to play. When visiting cities try to make time to wander around looking for events full of local colour. In a case like this your ears might suggest where to look.

Most major cities have areas that are particularly favoured by tourists, and London is no exception. Finding these spots is easy, but you will get a more interesting picture if you can also find a good vantage point and use a wide-angle lens to cover a greater area.

Sometimes one individual in a crowd can sum up all the charm of a race of people or the atmosphere of a town or region, such as in this picture taken in Sardinia.

If you want to depict local people in their own environment you may have to wait for a considerable time before outsiders step out of the picture and locals step into it. In the end a degree of compromise may be necessary, especially in places frequented by tourists.

A contemplative view of Amsterdam. The suggestion of human activity–the bicycle and the cart in the foreground–balance in both content and composition the broad sweep of the canal and the buildings reflected in it.

Below right: the photographer went in close for this picture of a stallholder in the Flea Market in Paris surrounded by a display of her wares.

Architecture and monuments

Buildings are notorious for not looking the same in pictures as they do in real life, largely because the human brain is far more tolerant of distortions in three dimensions than it is in two. It also has the capacity to overlook distracting elements such as people and their cars, dim light, telephone wires stretching across the sky and various transitory phenomena that assume an unintended permanence when fixed on photographic film.

Perspective, which makes parallel lines such as railway tracks appear to converge as they approach the horizon, adds depth to landscape pictures but introduces an unwelcome 'distortion' known as *converging verticals* to views of buildings taken from ground level. This is not really a distortion at all, as it reflects what the eyes actually see (although not what the brain perceives). To make buildings vertical in pictures the photographer has to find ways of keeping the walls of buildings vertical in the viewfinder, parallel with the edges of the frame. Do this by stepping back from the subject and keeping the camera level, not pointing above the horizontal. The foreground will occupy proportionately more of the picture, but make this interesting where possible by filling it with other compositional elements such as people (to add scale) or a road or track sweeping up to the building in question. A more unlikely method is to go up another building a short way away until the proportions of the subject become normal.

A satisfactory viewpoint may be difficult to find for other reasons. The lighting should do justice to the surface texture of the building which means waiting until the sun is sloping in at an angle or is diffused by a thin cloud cover. The clutter of everyday life also has no part in a permanent picture of some timeless monument, so parked cars, telegraph wires and so on should be excluded in as far as it is possible to do so. A long exposure (5-10 seconds) will cause pedestrians to vanish provided they continue to walk through the frame without stopping, but you will probably need to use neutral density filters to reduce the exposure value sufficiently, and colour balance may be affected in undesirable ways in exposures of more than 1 second.

The combined effects of these problems will mean that in many cases there will have to be compromise, and it is up to the photographer to decide which are the lesser evils to live with.

The sky can be improved in architectural photography by the use of a polarizing filter or, in black and white only, by the use of a yellow or orange filter; these will also have the effect of enhancing the texture of brick, stone or wood surfaces.

Exposure needs to be calculated carefully in photographs which contain a lot of sky area or white walls, or both. Take a reading from close enough to the building or monument in question to exclude the sky; if the walls are brilliant white take a reading from a shadowed area; otherwise try exposing at one stop more (or better still, 1, $1\frac{1}{2}$ and 2 stops more) than the metered exposure.

Opposite page, top: overcast daylight without strong shadows is best for recording detail in statues. A yellow or orange filter enhances the texture of stone in black and white pictures.

Opposite page, bottom: using a bridge or archway to frame other buildings is a useful compositional device when applied with imagination. The bridge here frames The Dakotas, the apartment block in New York where John Lennon lived.

Above left: absolute symmetry is best avoided because it usually fails to generate any interest. Far more intriguing to the eye is symmetry relieved by some other element, such as these milk bottles.

Below left and centre: two identical views of All Souls College, Oxford, taken on the same day, showing how a few hours can make a great difference to the quality of sunlight.

Above: water makes an excellent foreground for buildings, especially when it is calm enough to reflect detail in the architecture. This well-balanced photograph was taken in that much-photographed city, Venice.

Below: although often denounced as being technically a 'fault' the apparent convergence of vertical lines does not necessarily invalidate a picture—and the effect is sometimes impossible to avoid.

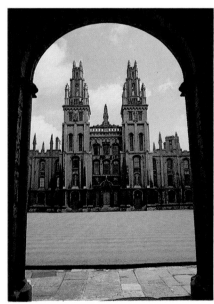

Interiors — architecture from within

It would be misleading to suggest that photographing interiors—as opposed to merely taking pictures indoors—is easy. It is quite difficult until you are used to it, the more so because the problems and pitfalls are not evident at first sight. However the techniques are worth the trouble of mastering because a well-photographed interior can be at least as interesting as an exterior shot of the same building and frequently more so. The two can be shown together to complement each other, adding another dimension to architectural photography which is often represented in amateur collections by a few more or less successful exterior photographs but no interiors.

A camera with a built-in exposure meter will often indicate that ambient interior light levels are too low for hand-held photography when pointing away from a window, and adequate when there is one included in the viewfinder. This is a literal statement of physics on the part of the exposure meter, not a true indication of whether or not the light is strong enough for photography. In these circumstances direct window light is often excessively contrasty—you may get a well-exposed picture of the window, but only a dim interior with deep shadows lacking in detail. Therefore ignore exposure meter readings influenced by direct daylight from a window. Meter only an area illuminated by reflected light, and if necessary abandon the idea of hand-held photography.

It is, in any case, almost always preferable to use a small aperture so as to gain maximum depth of field, and this necessitates the use of slow shutter speeds. A tripod and cable release are essential accessories therefore, and an adjustable camera with a B setting must be used.

Pocket and compact cameras with built-in flash or other fixed flash facilities are of use only in the very smallest of domestic interiors. The light from flash units falls off in intensity very rapidly, so that even a very powerful unit used on its own would be hopelessly inadequate to cope with a large-scale interior. (The techniques of photographing interiors by flash are described on pages 108-109.)

Colour film should be chosen with particular care. If normal daylight or tungsten films are used the photographer's scope will be severely limited by reciprocity failure (the effect by which colour emulsions on the same film react at a different rate when exposures last longer than about 1 second, resulting in inaccurate colour reproduction). Films can be

obtained which are manufactured especially for long exposures, mostly tungsten type B films available from larger photo stores.

Life will be easier for the specialist in interior photography if he can keep a separate camera loaded with long exposure type film. However, this is a luxury few people can afford. If the frame counter on a 35mm camera counts backwards when rewinding

it is fairly simple to wind a film back without losing the leader, so that you can change from one type to another in mid-film, returning to the place where you left off; otherwise colour-correction filters must be used to make tungsten type B films suitable for use in daylight (see page 54). The problem does not arise with 120 format SLRs having interchangeable film backs.

The interiors reproduced on these two pages were all taken without the aid of sophisticated equipment or materials. For a photograph such as that of the lunar module used in the first manned moon landing (opposite page, top) take care to expose for the subject and not for the window: point the camera away from the window to take a meter reading. The two church interiors were both taken by available light; for that on the opposite page the camera was hand-held, while for the one on the left it was carefully propped up on a pew for a one-second exposure (because it was important to get maximum depth of field). The bedroom (this page, top) was taken with a moderately wide-angle lens, such as is fitted as standard to many pocket cameras; but here again it was necessary to exclude the window from the viewfinder while taking a meter reading. The picture of the pipes (above) is the only one here not taken by available light: an electronic flash unit was used. In order to throw hard shadows behind the pipes and make them seem even more confused the flash was used off the camera, and direct rather than bounced or diffused.

Interiors (continued)

The problems described on the previous two pages may make interior photography sound rather daunting, but some aspects can be undertaken more easily without special films or filters.

Ceilings are sometimes neglected because it does not always occur to us to look up at them unless we know in advance that there is something noteworthy to look at. To photograph a ceiling, use a tripod or simply put the camera on the floor on its back. You will not be able to look through the viewfinder using the latter method, but provided the centre of

Right: an interior does not have to be a neat and tidy room, nor need it lack human interest. The clutter of the furniture restorer's workshop and the presence of the craftsman himself are of equal importance in this picture documenting a vanishing world.

Right: If you want to preserve the authentic colours of the light in interiors such as this amusement arcade, however garish and metallic they may be, keep to a daylight-type film and do not be tempted to illuminate the scene with flash—its colourless light would kill off the atmosphere. This limits you to using fast film for hand-held shots, but one of 400 ASA, together with a wide-angle lens, should make photography possible in all but the dimmest corners.

Below: another case where the use of flash is best avoided—the harshness of its light may be inappropriate in black and white photography as well as in colour.

Opposite page, left: a straightforward photograph of a stained glass window is quite easy to take. Expose for the glass itself, taking a meter reading from quite close up—do not allow a dim surround to affect the reading, or the coloured panes of glass may lose all their colour and character.

Opposite page, right: by tilting the camera downwards the photographer has deliberately introduced an unusual perspective to this almost abstract image, turning a mundane domestic interior into a quietly coloured geometric composition.

the ceiling is directly above and the camera is laid square-on the result should be satisfactory. The scene can be metered beforehand, and since it is not necessary to obtain extensive depth of field a wide aperture can be used, keeping exposures short. Keep well out of the way—if a wide-angle lens is fitted it is easy to come in at the side of the picture by mistake.

Stained glass windows make excellent subjects (particularly for colour transparencies) and are not difficult to photograph. The essential point is to move up to the glass when metering—do not meter the surrounding walls or the glass itself may be overexposed, resulting in an insipid brightness with thin, washed out colours. There must, of course, be light outside—preferably sunlight diffused by a thin but unbroken cloud cover. Best results are achieved if the camera is level with the centre of the window, although this may not be easy. A moderate telephoto lens may help to overcome this problem.

Flash can be used to illuminate interiors if it is of the type that can be used off the camera. Put the camera on a tripod at the back of the building, stop down to about f/11, open the shutter and lock it on the B setting.

Then you can illuminate the entire scene with a series of flashes aimed at the important points. Each separate flash should be made from a position hidden from the direct view of the camera, otherwise ghost silhouettes of the photographer and flash unit will be recorded on film; so make them while hiding behind pillars, buttresses, furniture and so on. Naturally enough this technique can only be used when there is very little ambient light in the building, and might be considered rather ill-advised if other members of the public are coming and going.

A wide-angle lens will be used more than any other for photographing interiors, because it gets more in; this also enhances the impression of spaciousness inside buildings. However there are times when a standard lens will do equally well, and for isolating out-of-reach details a telephoto will also be useful.

Beware of mixing different light sources; your film/filter combination will give correct colour reproduction with one type of source only. A shaft of daylight will have a most unpleasant blue cast if allowed to record on tungsten film; while a domestic lamp, if used to supplement daylight, will have a dull yellow-orange cast.

Portraits

It is of primary importance to achieve exactly the lighting effects you want when making a portrait of someone. For this reason many great portrait photographers usually work in a studio, where every element is under their control and nothing is left to chance. However, satisfactory portraits can be taken in the open air without the aid of elaborate equipment and props.

Direct sun is an extremely poor form of lighting for portraits; it is harsh and crude and lacks subtlety. When it shines into people's faces it causes them to squint, and throws hard shadows that contrast violently with the highlight areas. To make a portrait in bright sunny conditions use one of the following techniques: move your subject into the shade; turn him sideways-on to the direction of the sun and fill in shadows with a white reflector or with flash; turn his back to the sun and use fill-in flash to illuminate the face and eyes. The last technique is especially effective with beautiful girls because the sun, used

as backlighting, produces in the hair a radiant halo-like effect. Fill-in lighting is necessary, however, and a reflector is not suitable if it has to be held in front of the face, because it can dazzle the subject almost as much as the sun can.

There are no such problems if the sky is lightly overcast: the cloud layer diffuses the sun's rays and provides a much softer, more even lighting which is ideal for portraiture. In fact it is in conditions such as these that colour film (especially reversal film) reproduces life most faithfully; contrast is not too strong and the spectral composition of the light matches the daylight emulsions.

Taking portraits indoors by window light is not dissimilar to working out of doors. Direct sun coming through a window is strongly directional and will produce violent contrasts, so is best avoided. Position your subject in the shadows and use a reflector to throw a more diffuse light into the face; a white towel or sheet of paper or card will be perfectly satisfactory,

as will a beaded glass projection screen.

If there is a cloud cover or the sunlight is not shining in, a pleasant soft light can be obtained by moving the sitter away from the immediate vicinity of the window. The ambient light level may become too low for hand-held photography, so a longer

exposure should be made with the camera on a tripod.

A single artificial light or flash unit is enough for portraiture when there is no natural light or it is too weak to be of any value. The best position for such a light source is somewhat above, in front of and to one side of the subject's face—in other words roughly where the sun might be in mid-morning. A reflector should be used to fill in the shadows in exactly the same way as with sunlight. But better than this is to use a secondary light source—it is quite easy to arrange and rearrange two light sources until you get the effect you want. One should always be the main source; the other is used to fill in. If both are of the same type and wattage, move the secondary light twice as far from the subject as the primary one.

Use colour correction filters (see page 54) if you are not using a film balanced for the light source. Lighting is only one of the variable factors at the portrait photographer's disposal. The lighting arrangements described here presuppose a classical if somewhat unimaginative approach, and in practice it would certainly be a good idea to familiarize yourself with such basics before going on to explore some of the more 'interpretative' ways of illustrating a person's character.

Opposite page: strong sunlight can be too harsh for portraits, casting hard shadows and causing the subject to squint. A slightly overcast day (top) will produce better, less contrasty results and more faithful reproduction of skin tones. You cannot stop the sun shining, but you can often move your sitter into the shade (bottom left)—try to avoid the shade of brightly coloured objects as they will create an overall tint that discolours the skin. Bright daylight coming through a window can also be successfully used (bottom right): for a contrasty result go close to the window; for a softer approach move well away from it.

This page: an informal snapshot-portrait (top left) which also relies on even daylight to give detail in a relatively small subject, and colour has been faithfully recorded in the background. A more formal portrait can be taken by window light (top right) but a large white sheet of cardboard had to be used as a reflector to fill in the deep shadows on the right hand side of the picture. For the outdoor portrait (left) the combination of a fast shutter speed to freeze the movement of the subject's hair, which was blowing in the wind, and a wide aperture giving an out-of-focus background is the key to success.

Portraits (continued)

A standard approach is to photograph your sitter about three-quarters face to the camera, and with the eyes towards the top of the picture looking at the viewer. The picture would be upright—the vertical format is known as 'portrait' format in publishing terminology. But instead of doing this you can have the subject face-on to the camera—a direct, forceful approach—or in profile; the camera angle can be chosen such that the subject appears to be looking down at the viewer or looking up at him, the former tending to make an impression of dominance, the latter one of sub-missiveness. He can be surrounded by the things that are associated with him or that he symbolizes, or can be depicted against a plain background, the picture relying on expression alone for its impact.

These are just a few ideas mentioned to show that you do not have to take portraits (or any other type of picture) according to some formula. Think about your subjects before you begin to set up the camera, props and so on: decide which side of them you want to present to the world.

Once you have made up your mind how you wish to portray a person, work fast. Displaying confidence is not a uniquely photographic skill, but it is one which the portrait photographer needs if he is to get the best from his sitters; some of them, after all, may not like being photographed. Self-consciousness is the ruin of a portrait, and so the photographer must be able to make people feel relaxed.

There is, of course, no reason why portraits should always be posed. You can take pictures of people as they go about their daily lives—having a drink, playing games, asleep in a chair or fretting over some task or other; the informal portrait can reveal as much about a person as a formal one. Whatever approach you decide on,

take a good number of frames. The human face is extraordinarily mobile, and frozen at the wrong instant it can look quite contorted.

Avoid photographing people close up with wide-angle lenses unless you are deliberately trying to achieve a caricature effect. The human face is portrayed most accurately by a lens of rather longer than standard focal length—about 70-90mm with

Below left: the farmer and his wife, relaxing for a moment, are portrayed in the countryside of which they are a part. Background and subject are integrated and complementary, but the background is simple enough not to be distracting.

Below: the human figure depicted in this photograph is as much a part of the composition as an individual in his own right. Imagine how weak the composition would be if the figure were removed.

the 35mm film format—and anything shorter should be used with caution. A further property of telephoto lenses is that with their restricted depth of field, which is particularly marked at close focusing distances and wide apertures, they cause many backgrounds to be way out of focus. The effect can be enormously advantageous in portrait photography.

Below: for a really good portrait of a baby, go in close—fill the frame if you can. You may need someone else to help entertain him: here the baby was propped up on cushions and his mother stood ready with the camera while a bout of frantic gesticulations and face-pulling by his father was eventually rewarded with this bright smile. Close framing has naturally excluded all evidence of this. If he is facing the light source there will be a 'catch light' in the eyes of your sitter, which is worth remembering whatever his age, as it helps to add life and vitality to the whole face. With babies it is always recommended to take more than one photograph and select the best one for final enlargement.

Above: photographing people at work is a sure way of producing portraits that are informative as well as interesting, whether or not you know the subject. This photograph was lit by direct flash, but no other special techniques were needed.

Below: backlighting produces excellent results when properly used—sometimes it is difficult to get the exposure right. When it succeeds it is flattering to old and young alike. The dense background makes the effect even more striking.

Family photographs and other groups

A group portrait is not a number of individual pictures occurring within the same frame; it is a portrait of a number of people who have something in common, and the stranger looking at such a picture for the first time should be able to deduce what the link between them is.

Perhaps the term 'group portrait' is rather grandiose, suggesting stuffy Victorian family portraits or some cleverly posed gathering of art students. Here we are talking about something more down-to-earth: *relaxed* family photos, sports team photographs or a party giving a departing a colleague a send-off to remember.

To take a picture of the family at home you will need their patience and co-operation. With a number of people rather than a single individual it is much more difficult to photograph them without asking them to pose, however informally. Work out your plans and lighting arrangements before you trouble them, then tell them where you want them to stand or sit. If the group is large arrange the members in tiers – for example you could create three levels by having two or three people sitting on a sofa, two or three more (perhaps children) sitting or kneeling in front of it, and anything up to about half a dozen standing behind or around it: babies can, of course, be carried by their parents or by brothers and sisters.

Photofloods are by far the best light source for this kind of work as they can be combined and moved around to provide soft, even illumination over the entire gathering. Domestic lighting is a relatively poor substitute but can be used; with both types of lighting a tungsten film is essential. Flash is difficult to handle in circumstances such as these, and should only be used as a last resort.

Having the camera on a tripod makes the process easier and enables you to utilise the self-timer if you have one, giving you the chance to join the group yourself. Otherwise, to get yourself into the picture, you will need a long cable release with an air

bulb, which should be trailed across the floor out of the viewfinder area.

A sports team photograph should be taken out of doors on a slightly overcast day if possible. There are traditional ways of arranging the captain and players together with the implements of their sport, and these

Arrange groups of people in a number of tiers, according to the film format you are using. This photograph was originally taken to illustrate football club colours.

When travelling in a foreign country you cannot boss the natives around as you might your own family. Have the patience to wait until a pleasing arrangement forms naturally.

Right: a group such as this, with an obvious and absorbing common interest, can make a happy portrait—but the photographer needs an iron will to get them to stand still for long enough.

Below: photographing people from above is a way of introducing a note of humour, although it is a technique that can also be used for serious photography.

Bottom: for larger groups, formal or informal, a wide-angle lens can be an enormous asset. This group of office workers was taken with a 24mm lens—that is, one which takes in just over twice the area covered by a standard lens on a 35mm camera.

should be observed unless there is a particular reason to deviate from them, especially if the team portrait is an annual ritual.

Groups and party gatherings of moderate to large sizes can best be photographed out of doors, and again a slightly overcast day will solve all your lighting problems. Posing should be simple if the gathering has not specifically been convoked for photography: at tables people sitting near the camera can be asked to sit straight, the others leaning progressively further inwards with distance (the camera being positioned at one end of the table). Another good way to tackle social gatherings without bothering people too much or parting them from their drinks is to ask them to gather together and watch you photograph them from an upstairs window: the effect borders on the humorous without becoming flippant. If it is a birthday or leaving party or some similar celebration it is easy to make one person the focal point by asking the others to form a semicircle around him or her. Another advantage of this treatment is that it usually provides an unfussy background, and people's faces are not obscured by the tall hats etc.

A wide-angle lens makes group photography easier, especially in a confined space. The distortions can be grotesque if the group is too deep, however, so take care with this aspect of the composition.

Weddings

Successful wedding photography depends on a combination of many skills and disciplines described elsewhere in this book, but above all you need to know how to depict people to show them at their best, whether singly, in pairs or in groups; posing or behaving naturally; in all places and in conditions both favourable and unfavourable.

Do not try to supplant the professional wedding photographer. By all means photograph the same groups and situations, but let him use his experience and special equipment to set up the main formal picture sequence. Keep out of his way, and on no account contradict his instructions to the bride and groom and their families.

The following are important traditional wedding scenes. The bride should be pictured full-length in her dress before leaving for the church; for a natural-looking pose at this

nervous moment ask her to hold the bouquet with both hands. Photograph her getting into and/or out of the car, and being accompanied to the church porch. Do not take pictures in church unless you have obtained prior permission to do so; it is not always permitted, although sometimes it is only the use of flash units that is discouraged. If you do have permission, take pictures of the couple at the altar, signing the register and then coming down the aisle.

The pictures outside the church can include the bride and groom on their own, the bride with the bridesmaids, the groom with the best man, the bride and groom with their parents, then with all the members of the immediate families, then the entire company; some or all of these permutations can be employed, but there is no reason why you should not use others if the couple and their family want them.

At the reception take pictures of all the speakers, the couple cutting the cake, the guests raising their glasses for toasts, the wedding presents if they are on display; also take plenty of pictures of the bride and groom circulating among the guests, and try to get in as many different faces as you can—ideally every guest should appear in at least one photograph.

Finally there is the scene as bride and groom leave for their honeymoon. Try to get one of the bride throwing her bouquet away.

There is no second time around with weddings, so if you are

There are some pictures which should not be missed in any sequence of wedding photographs. These include a full-length picture of the bride in her wedding dress (below left), for which particular care is needed not to underexpose because of the brilliant whiteness of the material, and (below right) nervous moments for the groom and the best man.

approached by friends or relations to act as official photographer, do not accept without first considering the consequences should you have an off-day. If you do agree to do the job, you should have at least a 35mm format camera—preferably a single-lens reflex—a powerful flash unit and plenty of film. A standard or moderately wide-angle lens will be the most useful.

It is important not to skimp on film, because if a vital photograph is spoiled by some unpredictable occurence—a momentarily unflattering facial expression, for example —it is impossible to go back and shoot it again. Take *at least* two pictures of the important moments, and more if you are in any doubt about the success of one of them. Plan the whole thing in advance, do not expect just to wander in on it like a casual snapshotter. Do the bride and groom have any special requirements —romantic soft-focus pictures perhaps, or an interior photograph of the church when empty? And find out what the arrangements are in the event of rain spoiling the day.

Above: a traditional wedding group. Never try to economise on film when taking wedding photographs, particularly if the couple are relying on you for their main set of pictures —which is not a task to be lightly undertaken. When a number of people have to look their best at the same time it is essential to take two or three exposures at the very least.

Below left: keep an eye open for moments which capture the atmosphere of a wedding day, but which do not form part of the formal sequence.

Below: a wedding is an important occasion for the bridesmaids, too, so do not neglect them. Page boys, ushers, immediate and not-so-immediate families—try to get them all into the pictures at least once.

Theatre, circus and other shows

There are specific problems to overcome when taking photographs from an auditorium at a public performance or show. The most evident is that you cannot easily move around without disturbing other members of the audience, and so you have to make the best of a single viewpoint, which will almost certainly not be the one you would have chosen. In public theatres photography may not be permitted at all during the performance, and this restriction should never be disregarded; however, one or two pictures may sometimes be taken during applause, curtain calls or other noisy moments. The nature of the lighting on a stage, arena or circus ring also creates certain problems.

Anyone with a particular interest in photographing theatre would be well advised to approach a local amateur dramatic society. Unless they already have a regular photographer they will probably be glad to let you photograph one or two rehearsals; in these circumstances they may not mind you moving around in the front rows, or even among the actors if you build up a good relationship with the company, and they may be tolerant of flash if it is limited to one or two sessions. In return you could offer them prints of the best pictures. One or two tableaux and perhaps portrait studies of the leading players would provide them with a documentary record of their productions. For more atmospheric theatre shots go backstage before and during the dress rehearsal—the possibilities here are endless.

To create good images representing particular productions you will need to be familiar with the script of the play, with the relationships between the main characters and the producer's own interpretation of them. Read the play and sit in on one or two rehearsals before you begin photographing: you will then be able to anticipate the moments of maximum drama and significance, and have your equipment ready and in the right place to capture them.

At any spectacle which has to be

The Royal Shakespeare Company rehearsing for a production of Romeo and Juliet. Do not let a large dense area of shadowed background influence your camera to overexpose spotlit parts of the scene; and if working with colour transparency film, choose one balanced for tungsten lighting.

If you can establish links with an amateur theatre group you may be permitted to photograph on stage during rehearsals. If you are familiar with the work being produced you will be able to anticipate the crucial moments.

viewed from a fixed position—including the theatre if it is at a performance rather than a rehearsal—it will help if you have a choice of lenses: a wide-angle to take in the entire scene, including the wings and the silhouetted heads of the audience in the front rows, and a telephoto to take you right into the centre of the action if your seat is too far back for standard lens shots. Do not use flash at public performances of plays, concerts and any other entertainments requiring concentration on the

part of the audience. Unless you are in one of the front rows it will do little good in any case, merely serving to add highlights to the hair of people sitting in front of you: flash light falls off much too rapidly to illuminate a distant stage or circus ring.

Exposure metering can be difficult at stage spectacles because of the concentrated nature of the light and the contrast between spotlit highlights and areas of dense shadow. The most reliable method is to use a hand-held spot meter; failing this, through-the-lens metering with a telephoto lens will give a sufficiently accurate reading which should be retained when you change to other lenses, using manual override if the camera is automatic. Do not be surprised if meter readings seem to indicate a light level that is much lower than you anticipated; the eye perceives theatrical lighting as being brighter than it actually is. With 400 ASA film an exposure of 1/30 second at f/8 will probably be about right. Try underexposing a few when you are getting used to this sort of photography—you may find that harsh highlights amid pools of dense black shadow convey a sense of the occasion that is to your taste.

The kind of lighting that you are likely to encounter from one show to the next will vary in intensity and colour, so it is impossible to lay down strict rules about film/filter combinations. In general tungsten film will give the best results. Although the interchangeable lens facility will be indispensable at times, single-lens reflex cameras are somewhat noisy in comparison with compact and rangefinder types, and this may make them awkward to use at certain moments.

Top right: grotesque portrait of a clown, taken with a telephoto lens in Chicago, USA.

Right: the multicoloured lights used in discotheques will look strange and lurid whatever film is used—there is no point in trying to compensate for the effect by using tungsten film. Go instead for speed: use a 400 ASA film possibly uprated to 800 ASA.

Action and movement

Some of the subjects discussed and illustrated on these pages are essentially static: landscape, flowers, architecture, still life—these subjects are devoid of action in themselves and their treatment in photography reflects this. In reality all things change eventually of course, but this consideration is irrelevant here: they are portrayed photographically as being immobile, eternal if you like.

Other subjects demand a completely different approach: one that conveys movement, flow, flux and change, slow or fast, on a gigantic or microscopic scale. Photography has two ways of meeting these requirements: the first is to 'freeze' the essence of the movement in an instant of maximum tensile power; the second is to allow time for the continuing process of change to record on film. Put more simply, a fast shutter speed can be chosen to stop movement or a slow one can be used to blur it. Which of these methods is chosen depends partly on the subject and partly on the photographer's personal approach to it. They can also be combined in the same image by the use of techniques such as panning (see page 122) and double exposure.

The shutter speed necessary to stop dead a moving object depends on the speed at which it is moving. An exposure of 1 second will be fast enough to stop (or more correctly, to create the illusion of stopping) really slow-moving objects such as drifting clouds, shadows cast by the sun, smoke rising into the air, and so on. But to stop a passing train, a ball thrown into the air, or the flight of a bird will require a much faster job of work by the camera—an exposure of perhaps 1/500 or 1/1000 second (imagine sorting through a thousand pictures of the same thing taken within the space of one second).

To allow movement to record on film the limits of photography have to be stretched in the opposite direction: a running athlete's arms and legs will begin to blur at exposures of around 1/125 or 1/60 second; the time needed to record significant movement in the clouds may be anything from a few seconds to several minutes, while the apparent motion of the stars in the night sky can be recorded for as long as the sky is not lit by the sun or moon—for several hours if conditions are favourable. (Again it has to be pointed out that time exposures can only be made with a camera that can be mounted on a tripod and its shutter locked on the B setting.)

The photographer must choose between these approaches or com-

Above: the techniques of panning and prefocusing had to be employed simultaneously in the picture of a little girl overawed by the noise and the sweep and turn of the merry-go-round. Prefocusing was necessary because of the wide aperture that had to be used in the low light—note how severely restricted depth of field is.

Left: panning a police car as it swerved round a corner has resulted in an unusual variation on the familiar motion-blur effect. The fact that the car windscreen is pin-sharp testifies to the photographer's skill in following a moving subject, while the unmistakable sense of movement conveys the high drama of a movie car chase.

Above: movement is suggested here not by a blurred and streaked background such as panning produces, but by composition alone–the mind insists that the little girl cannot stay suspended in the air in this diagonal position. A fast shutter speed must be used to freeze motion in this way.

Below: a slow shutter speed has allowed the train to move during the exposure. One of the effects of perspective in cases such as this is to maximise movement in the parts of the subject that are nearest to the camera, and minimise it in the parts that are farthest away.

Above: another example of panning with prefocusing. The motion evident from both the streaked background and the tractor wheel, combined with the strong diagonal composition, give this picture a quality of almost physical directness–it is as if the tractor driver is about to tumble headlong out of the frame.

bine them if he wants his pictures to suggest movement. He can then make them even more effective by using certain tricks of composition. Strong diagonals, especially within a vertical frame, set up a feeling of dynamic tension, and a top-heavy distribution of dark areas creates a feeling of imbalance. Instinctively the mind wants these tensions to be resolved, to settle into an orderly pattern. The skilful photographer knows how to exploit these subconscious responses, sometimes even to the extent that a landscape, silent and immobile in reality, can be turned into a torrent of conflicting forces in the photographic image.

Sports — a question of timing

At its highest level this is an extremely specialized branch of photography, and one which requires sophisticated and enormously expensive pieces of equipment as well as patience, dedication and imagination on the part of the photographer.

At a more modest level sports scenes can be undertaken with any equipment, including pocket cameras and compacts, but if you intend to take more than the occasional snapshot of the school sports day or a bit of football practice in the garden, you have little alternative to arming yourself with a 35mm single-lens reflex camera. You will need to add to the basic body and 50mm lens combination as and when your budget allows.

In the majority of sports pictures the action is frozen. Anyone can freeze action if they have a camera which is capable of shutter speeds in the region of 1/500 or 1/1000 second. The skill of the photographer is in identifying the essential moment that says most about the sport in question, and having identified the moment, to capture *exactly* that moment on film—not a microsecond before or after it. There will be alternative views—no single image can sum up every aspect of a particular sport—and the true enthusiast will

want to photograph the personalities as well as the events, so that pictures of sportsmen performing the same actions or gestures may not be as repetitive as they would look to a complete outsider.

To photograph the precise moment when the racket makes contact with the ball, the boxing glove with the face or when the goalkeeper is suspended in mid-air you will need to develop a faultless sense of timing: you have to anticipate the moment and press the shutter release in advance, by a very slight but definite interval. Imagine a ball thrown high

into the air: to photograph it at the moment it reaches its highest point you would need to release the shutter just *before* it stops rising; delay until the moment arrives and the ball will already be on its way down when the exposure is made.

In some sports there are fewer peaks, the action being continuous rather than a series of brief, intense bursts. Most races belong in this category. In this case the sport is better represented by the motion-blur technique called *panning*—following the subject in the camera viewfinder and using a shutter speed

Top right: a fast shutter speed has frozen the motion both of the surfer and of the waves with their crests of spray being whipped off by the wind. At the same time a long telephoto lens has been used to magnify the rather distant subject and bring it closer in to the photographer. The picture conveys some of the excitement of the sport.

Right: the first moments in free fall are caught in this exhilarating photograph of skydivers launching themselves into the void. It was taken with a helmet-mounted single-lens reflex like the one worn by the skydiver on the right of the picture. Although such specialized equipment is not cheap to buy, it may be available for hire.

slow enough to blur the background but fast enough to stop the main subject itself. This technique will need some practice, preferably with an empty camera to start with, then with one or two trial black and white films. With a standard lens start at 1/125 second for the fastest subjects and 1/60 for slower ones, going down to 1/60 and 1/30 when you have mastered the technique. Panning with a telephoto lens becomes more and more difficult in proportion with focal length, but the results can be really spectacular when a shot succeeds.

There is another technique that the sports photographer should be able to call on at will. Known as *prefocusing* this involves focusing the camera on a spot where you know the contestants will pass—e.g. the finishing line—and waiting until they get there before making the exposure. This technique is useful when the contestants are approaching the photographer head-on or nearly so, as it obviates the need to alter focus from one instant to the next.

With both panning and prefocusing the action of releasing the shutter should be perfectly smooth, especially with long lenses, and you should follow through after the exposure (unless in prefocusing there is no lateral movement to follow).

A telephoto lens—better still a range of telephoto lenses or a zoom—is of tremendous value to the sports photographer, as it will enable him to get into the centre of the action from considerable distances. The advantages and limitations of telephoto lenses are described in more detail on pages 138-139.

Modern fast films have also extended the range of conditions in which the sports photographer can operate successfully: colour films rated at 400 ASA are commonly available and can be push-processed to 800 ASA (at extra cost if commercially undertaken), while in black and white work the availability of Kodak Recording Film, rated at 1000 ASA, makes action photography possible in very dim conditions. Grain is rather evident if negatives are enlarged to great sizes, but this is a small price to pay for the additional benefits this film brings to sports photography.

Fast films not only make photography possible in dim light, they also allow the photographer the option of selecting a faster shutter speed in bright light or a small aperture for good depth of field, and there are times when both of these are vital in sports photography.

Above: the leaning position of the brightly clad figures is sometimes the only outward sign of the intense effort going into trials of brute strength such as the tug of war. If the photographer had been able to get closer he could perhaps have captured some of the agonized determination contorting the faces of the participants; but it required a telephoto lens even to get this close.

Below and below left: good examples of the technique of panning to create an impression of speed. This may need some practice, but it is a skill which every serious sports photographer must be able to draw on whenever he needs it.

Wildlife and zoos

Natural history photography is one of the most absorbing and challenging of all specialist disciplines, requiring of its practitioners a greater range of skills than even sports photography. In zoos and wildlife parks the photographer whose equipment is less specialized can still practise some of the same skills; nevertheless for anything beyond the most basic work a 35mm single-lens reflex camera is a necessity. Ideally you would also pack a range of telephoto lenses up to 500mm or even 1000mm, at least one of which should have a macro facility, but a small selection together with a X2 telephoto converter is more economical of both money and space. If you are going to work out of doors in difficult conditions you should get an ultraviolet filter for each one of your lenses to provide permanent protection against dust and the elements.

The first rule of wildlife photography, whatever the circumstances, is to consider the welfare of the animal before your own. Many natural history photographers are biologists first and photographers second and will not need reminding of this; but others, enthusiastic amateurs with the best of intentions, can destroy an animal's habitat and interfere with its breeding behaviour with dire consequences for the species concerned. Therefore do not pursue wild animals unless you have a thorough understanding of the behaviour of the species. And *never* take a plant, animal or egg home for photography in controlled conditions.

When driving through a safari park keep the car windows shut: this is for your own safety. Do not wind them down for photography, however tempting it may be to do so. If the windows are cleaned before your visit and you push your lenses right up to the glass you will be able to take pictures through the windows with only negligible loss of quality. This is particularly true with telephoto lenses.

The bars or netting of cages in the zoo can be blurred to such an extent that they are virtually undetectable in photographs: the longer the lens and the closer it is to the obstructing bars, the more complete will be the success of this technique.

For close-up work with butterflies and other insects a tripod and electronic flash unit will be necessary, or better still, a macro lens with ring flash. For more about the techniques and equipment needed for close-up work see pages 60-61.

Photographing birds presents special problems whether they are at the nest or on the wing. Ideally you should build a hide in the vicinity of the nest. This must be done slowly so that the birds are not aware of any change in their environment. Birds in the air will have to be panned—a technique requiring plenty of practice even if the intention is not necessarily to blur the background for effect, as it is in sports photography.

Underwater photography is yet another subdivision of the subject. At an advanced level it means expensive cameras and attachments once again, however there are cheaper alternatives for the amateur who wishes to try it out before committing himself financially; e.g. the Minolta Weather-

Opposite page, top: caged animals can be photographed with little difficulty if you have a telephoto lens. A 135mm lens was used for this picture of a lion in the zoo, enabling the photographer to achieve a close-up effect. The shallow depth of field is characteristic of telephoto lenses used at short focusing distances.

Opposite page, bottom: another telephoto lens shot, this time taken not in the zoo, but in the African bush.

Above left: strongly directional side-lighting has lifted the swan right out of its watery background. The picture is perfectly framed and displays an impeccable sense of timing.

Above right: apes are wayward animals and you may need to use patience to get a good picture of one.

Below: a hippopotamus emerging from an African river—not as funny as it looks, but a telephoto lens enabled the photographer to keep a safe distance.

matic A is a 110 pocket camera that remains watertight down to a depth of 5 meters (15ft) below the surface, which is plenty for investigating the seashore and shallow seas.

Most serious natural history work is in colour because colour is often of biological importance, and on transparency film because this is the type preferred for reproduction in books and journals. Since high resolution and accurate colour are of vital importance, the slowest films that are still compatible with other requirements are most often used: many 35mm photographers use the slowest Kodachrome (25 ASA) when possible. At other times, such as when the long lenses have to be used, it is better to use a faster film (200-400 ASA) because of its greater adaptibility to different conditions.

Space permits only a few general points here; but there are some excellent books on the subject of natural history photography, and anyone who considers specializing in this rewarding area can invest in one of these.

Still life

Still life is a subject area which, for all its apparent simplicity, taxes a photographer's inventiveness and skill to no small degree. He needs to be thoroughly familiar with his equipment and the characteristics of his materials, in order to be able to visualize final results and achieve exactly (not approximately) the effects he has planned in his mind's eye. He should be sufficiently in control to be able to produce completely neutral, shadowless photographs of reasonably small objects. To combine this objectivity with a degree of abstraction is one of the aims of much still life photography.

Start by experimenting on a table top with a number of articles linked by a common theme, e.g. a bottle of wine, a bunch of grapes, a glass and a corkscrew; alternatively a selection of fruits or vegetables in a trug—anything provided it is not complicated or unwieldy. Arrange the chosen

Below left: one of a series of photographs taken at different exposures to be sure of striking the right balance between retaining detail in the dark blue glass and preserving the delicate pastel colours in the clear bottle to the right.

Below: the polished, gleaming metal of a car engine photographed with a wide-angle lens. Lighting was a combination of overcast daylight and, on the left, fluorescent strip lighting—this accounts for the greenish highlights on that side.

elements in different permutations, and each time you achieve a pleasing arrangement move the lighting unit or units around to create as many different effects as you can think of. Look at the whole setup often through the viewfinder of your camera during this process, whether or not you actually want to take a picture, in order to assess the visual impact of different subject arrangements and lighting.

To achieve certain effects you may want to illuminate the elements of the

Opposite page, top: an arrangement of fresh vegetables and fruit is an ideal subject if you wish to experiment with still life photography. In this case the vegetables were piled up on a dark brown blanket, sprayed with water to give them a fresh look, and lit by an ordinary table lamp with a metal reflector. A beaded glass projection screen (out of the picture to the left) provided a soft fill-in lighting, while a large book shaded the background. The film used was Ektachrome 160, balanced for tungsten lighting. The whole setup was extremely crude to look at, but it is only what appears in the finished picture that matters.

Below: for maximum detail in inanimate subjects the light should be soft and not too directional. But this need not be difficult to achieve —this picture is lit by available daylight from a window. For a similar soft effect you should choose a window facing away from the sun or take the pictures on an overcast day.

Above: like the picture below, this one was taken by available window light. Here, however, direct sun has been used to maximise contrast and diminish detail in the shadow areas. Exposing for the highlights has caused the shadows to drop into solid black, so that the earthenware pot appears to be floating in nothing.

subject from below, using a sheet of glass or perspex instead of a table top; you may also want reflectors— coloured or plain black or white—and background materials to be hung around the subject. No matter how much your creation might outwardly resemble one of Heath Robinson's famous contraptions, do not worry as long as this does not show in the final image.

At the mechanical level, be careful to choose an aperture that provides adequate depth of field to keep the subject in focus front to back, and to balance film with light source. If you want some ideas, look at the advertising photographs in magazines and on hoardings, and at book jackets and record covers, and try to work out what the photographer was trying to demonstrate with his still life picture, and what methods he must have used to achieve it. You could also try producing photographic equivalents of still life paintings—this would test your ingenuity. But the most rewarding pictures are the ones you conceive in your imagination and then recreate on photographic film.

Special effects — some simple tricks

Some uncomplicated special effects that are not beyond the scope of most amateurs are illustrated on this and the next page. These are all camera techniques—they can be used without resorting to manipulation of the image in the darkroom. Anyone who is particularly interested in this branch of photography could also investigate the possibilities offered by the ranges of special effects filters available today (see page 67).

Infra-red film

Films sensitive to radiation below the red end of the spectrum exist in both black and white and colour versions. Colour infra-red film distorts colours in unpredictable and rather surreal ways—it is also called 'false colour' infra-red. The black and white type is more predictable in some of its effects: it blackens blue sky and turns living foliage white, giving it a cherry-blossom appearance from a distance. These films are not available in 110 and 126 formats.

Double exposure

Most modern small-format cameras have a one-stroke film advance system which cocks the shutter at the

Right: two transparencies mounted in the same frame. The snow scene was taken on a 35mm compact with a 40mm lens; the sun was taken with a 200mm lens on an SLR, as described in the text.

Below: double exposure, combined with the use of a special effects filter. The filter was a simple mask with a hole in it; the effects of such devices may vary with lens aperture and so it is difficult to use them except with reflex viewing systems.

Below right: this curious illusion is in fact straight photography, the top half of the image being mirrored in a glass-topped table.

same time as winding the film on to the next frame. This linkage ensures that double exposures cannot be unwittingly made; but some cameras boast a special double/multiple exposure facility, and if yours is one of these you can create a number of startling double images. If your camera does not have this feature similar effects can be obtained by the use of electronic flash provided that it can be used off the camera. With the shutter locked open on the B setting in a completely or almost completely blacked-out room, you can fire a flash unit two or more times from the same position, moving or removing people or inanimate objects in between flashes. The estimated normal lens aperture should be reduced by one stop each time the number of flashes is doubled. The effect of double flash is to create 'ghost' images.

A similar technique can be used to photograph a person or thing twice on to the same piece of film without creating the ghost effect. Using an absolutely black background (e.g. by pointing the camera at an open

window on a moonless and starless night, tilting it slightly upwards if necessary), and with the camera locked on the B setting, position the subject in one half of the image area and fire the flash; then reposition the subject in the previously vacant area and fire the flash a second time. Provided there is no overlap of the images and that the flash is fired from the same spot, the trickery is undetectable.

Sandwiching transparencies
Mounting two transparencies in the same frame is a technique that can sometimes be used to cause strange optical illusions and add interest to certain dull shots. An interesting sky can be superimposed on an ordinary landscape, and foreground silhouettes on background shots lacking in depth. The transparencies have to be compatible, however, and one way to ensure this is to take at least some especially for the purpose. Next time the sun is shrouded in mist and only just definable, take one or two pictures of it with your telephoto lenses, overexposing it to get thin slides, and keeping the sun itself near

A double self-portrait such as this is simple to create if you have a lockable cable release and a camera with a B setting. Other than that you only need a darkened room and a dark background (in this case a blanket). With the camera locked open the two exposures were made simply by turning a table lamp on and off twice. To do this in colour you would need a film balanced for tungsten lighting, unless you are using a flash unit as described in the text.

the top of the picture area. You will then be able to add a disproportionately large sun to an otherwise drab landscape or cityscape, creating a science fiction scene. (*Never* look at the sun through telephoto lenses on a clear day: this may damage your eyesight.)

Rejected exposures from a bracketed sequence make good materials to experiment with. You can have particularly successful effects copied on to a single piece of film—negative or transparency—to make a definitive version; then, if you like, you can re-use the components.

Mounting, viewing and storing slides

A collection of slides may be a photographer's most valuable asset in financial as well as sentimental terms, and deserves to be handled and stored with care.

Mounting

Commercially processed reversal films are normally returned cut and mounted in either cardboard or plastic glassless frames. They will be returned unmounted in strips if it is specified that this is required, but mounting your own slides introduces an extra handling stage and with it the risk of damaging or fingerprinting the emulsion. Some photographers prefer to use glass mounts for the additional protection they offer, and this must be done at home. The two halves of the mount simply clip together, sandwiching the film. Glass mounts are relatively expensive, however, and moisture can become trapped between the glass and the film. Irregularly shaped rings in rainbow colours (known as Newton rings) can also form on the glass. Most photographers dispense with the use of glass mounts for these reasons, but great care must be taken not to touch the emulsion when a slide is handled.

Viewing

The best way to show a slide is in a darkened room with a projector and screen: in these circumstances

Top: it is now quite common for slide projectors to have an automatic focusing mechanism—the user has to focus the first of the sequence and after that it is done electronically. The Zeiss Ikon Autofocus has this facility, as well as a tape recorder control socket and remote control slide advance or reverse capability.

Centre: two projectors and a cross-fading set. This is a relatively expensive but impressive setup which would give a professional air to your slide shows. Such equipment can often be hired.

Right: a hand viewer is a simple, convenient and economical piece of equipment, and it can easily be used in daylight. Some models are mains convertible although most are operated by batteries.

photography gives of its best, with brilliant highlights, vivid colour reproduction and a window-on-the-world kind of immediacy that no other form of presentation can match. However, a projector and screen setup is expensive, and many rooms cannot be adequately darkened during the day.

As a cheaper substitute for the projector and screen (but preferably in addition to it) a hand viewer can be used. A number of models are available, some battery and some mains operated; some stack the slides and others have to be individually loaded. Although the image is not as impressive as that obtained with a projector, and cannot be easily viewed by more than one person at a time, the hand viewer makes slides (a) more portable, (b) viewable in daylight, and (c) more convenient to arrange in preparation for a full-scale slide show.

The simplest hand viewer consists of a translucent screen at the back of a tube with a magnifying lens at the front; the slide is illuminated by window or lamp light, with the viewer held up to the eye.

People who need to lay out a number of slides side by side for purposes of comparison or selection use a light box or slide sorting desk, which is a box with a translucent top illuminated from inside, together with a hand lens.

Storing slides

Commercially available systems for storing slides include magazine containers, which house slides in the same magazines as are used in the projector, and filing sheets, which can be bought for use in metal filing cabinets or in ring binders. The advantage of the filing sheet is that a number of slides can be displayed at the same time without individual handling.

Slides should never be stored in damp or hot conditions, especially if they are kept in the processors' plastic boxes. And if stored loose in drawers or on shelves they will collect dust, scratches and finger marks and will soon be of no interest whatever to anyone.

Below: 35mm transparencies arranged in sequence for projection. Setting up a slide show should be done with as much care as compiling an album so that the viewer's interest is maintained from one frame to the next. The sequence should ideally be varied but not fragmentary: try to mix long shots with close-ups, scenic pictures with action shots, vertical with horizontal, brilliant colours with muted ones, and so on. Avoid very violent contrasts unless you are deliberately setting out to give your audience a jolt, but above all keep them awake—pictures with the subject in more or less the same proportions very quickly become monotonous, however good they may be technically. Transparencies cannot be cropped in the same way as prints, but black tape can be used to mask them if there is obtrusive clutter at the edges. A range of masks is commercially available, including circles, squares and rectangles in various sizes, and these can be effective when used with suitable slides.

1

2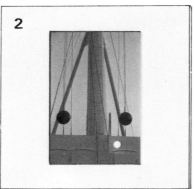

3

4

5

6

Your album — make it interesting

Filling a photograph album with a lot of pictures all of the same size, some good and some bad, may be enough to stir the photographer's memory of his holiday, but is unlikely to interest anyone else. Think of your album as a book which you are trying to sell to other people: it has to be lively and interesting, or no one will buy it.

There is no need to tell a story in the anecdotal sense, but there should be a sense of flow, or of the subjects being thematically connected. Sticking prints in at random robs them of their impact and does little justice to any photographic skills they display.

Vary the pace from one page to the next. Careful juxtaposition of different print sizes will arrest attention, whereas a uniform presentation will lull your viewers agreeably to sleep. Have some big enlargements made of the very best pictures and give each one a page to itself. Also vary the number and layout of smaller prints, letting the qualities of the photographs dictate whether they harmonize or contrast with the contents of the preceding and following pages in terms of subject matter, colour, composition and so on.

Some people like to combine their pictures with mementos other than purely photographic ones. Travel tickets, wedding invitations, children's drawings—anything that will lie flat can be used if you favour this approach, even photographs taken by other people if they are good enough. This is of course more appropriate for souvenir albums and personal records than for a photographic showcase, but there is no reason why you should not compile two or more albums simultaneously.

Consider whether it is worth giving individual prints a caption or legend. 'Sally with Jean-Pierre, Champs Elysées 1904' would be enough to ensure that you do not forget names and places as the years roll by.

Albums are available ready bound or as ring binders into which you insert your own pages. The latter type is more adaptable, although you have to mount the prints yourself.

Filing the negatives

Keep negatives in the paper sleeves made for the purpose. Do not neglect this, because you never know when a favourite print may get damaged or lost, or when someone else may ask for a copy of one. If you accumulate a lot of negatives transfer them to one of the paper sheets made to be filed in a ring binder (taking seven strips of six 35mm negatives or four of 6 × 6cm). For reference purposes a contact sheet can be punched with holes and filed next to the negatives to facilitate the business of finding specific pictures later on.

Store negative files in a safe place with a free circulation of air, and away from excessive heat, cold or humidity.

Opposite page: the leaves of a photograph album will look more lively if you vary the proportions and layout of the pictures, and if spreads are thematically connected rather than being a disjointed succession of prints. Have a few of your very best photographs enlarged, and do not be afraid to crop if this improves the composition. You can crop when printing if you do your own; commercial processing houses may also do this but you should make your instructions to them as clear and detailed as possible. Another method is to trim prints using a handyman's knife and a metal ruler— sometimes you may even be able to cut one ordinary sized print into two smaller ones. If the content of a picture is predominantly pale, giving it a black border often helps to hold the subject together and supply a professional finishing touch: do this with a technical drawing pen (available from drawing office supplies or graphic arts shops).

Below: negative files, showing paper negative sleeves for 6 × 6cm ($2\frac{1}{4} \times 2\frac{1}{4}$in) and 35mm negatives. If the negatives are filed together with a contact sheet as shown here, locating any given negative in the future will be a much easier task.

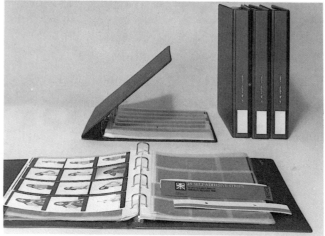

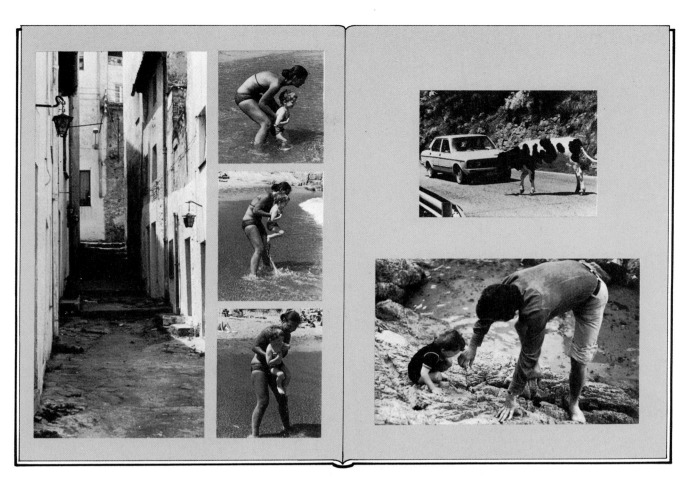

Prints for the wall — retouching, mounting and framing

Prints which are to be displayed individually will have more visual impact if they are mounted on to a piece of blockboard or stiff card.

Choose a background colour that will show the print to its best advantage: neutral colours such as grey or buff are generally the most suitable, although black or white can be used for pictures with a sufficiently strong graphic element. Use a card that is large enough to allow a generous border around the print, and more below than on top; while this can easily be trimmed later if the borders are too large, the reverse process is impossible and both print and mount will have to be discarded if the mount is too small.

The best and most permanent method of mounting a print is by means of adhesive tissue and a dry mounting press; however this is a fairly elaborate piece of equipment and so unless you can join a photographic club and share the use of one, you may prefer to use either rubber cement or a special print mountant not requiring the use of a press.

Rubber cement should be applied thinly and evenly to both surfaces and allowed to dry for 10-15 minutes. After drying the two surfaces will adhere on contact, so make sure the print is exactly in position before pressing down gently, starting at one corner and working outwards from the centre in a leaf-skeleton pattern. Make sure that no air bubbles form. Surplus cement around the edges can be rubbed off with the fingers. Pictures fixed with rubber cement can be loosened with solvent if necessary.

With the thermal mountant marketed for photographic use you can match the effectiveness of the dry mounting system without having to use a press. Temperature is less critical than with adhesive tissue, so a domestic iron can be used instead.

By either method a number of prints can be mounted on to the same piece of board, although you should choose prints which have the same paper surface and are compatible in colour balance.

Both black and white and colour prints can be retouched to conceal minor imperfections and blemishes. Retouching kits are available consisting of watercolours for filling white marks left by dust on the negative, and a scraping knife for removing black marks from black and white prints.

When retouching a colour print the colour has to be matched with great care if the job is to be invisible, but with patience, a steady hand and a good magnifying glass some dramatic improvements can be effected. It is easier to work on mounted prints than unmounted ones.

For an especially impressive finish make a mask for your mounted prints and cover them with picture glass and a frame. Framing kits are obtainable from craft centres. A more expensive alternative for a de-luxe finish is to have the job done commercially; a cheap way is to buy an old frame, with or without a picture it, at a junk shop, and make the print to fit the frame instead of the frame to fit the print.

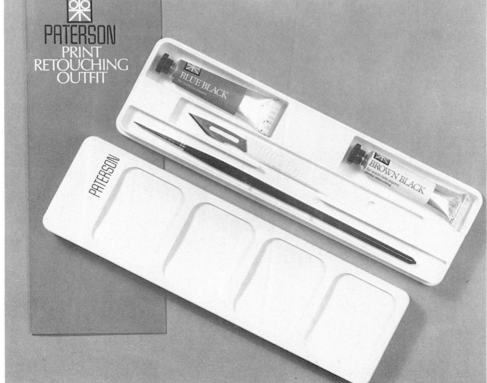

Opposite page, top: framing a print gives it a distinguished look, and need not be expensive.

Opposite page, bottom: if a negative has been mishandled or badly stored it may accumulate marks which show in the prints. Careful retouching can conceal this, although for a really good, almost invisible finish it must be painstakingly carried out.

Left: a Paterson print retouching kit.

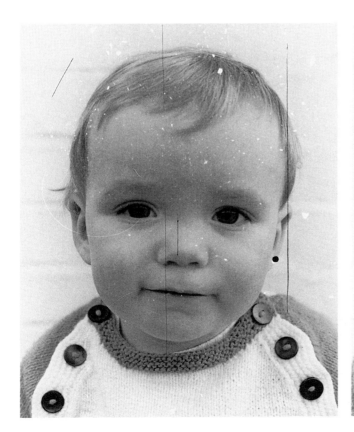 

Tripods and other camera supports

Of all the additional pieces of equipment that the photographer can buy once he has a camera with adjustable shutter speeds, perhaps the most useful is a good solid tripod. This is too often underrated by amateurs who, anxious to increase the scope of their photography, will go out and recklessly spend money on impressive mirror or macro lenses, filter holders, teleconverters or other bits of glamorous-looking paraphernalia.

This is not to say that all of these things do not have their uses, only that they are often limited in their practical applications. But a tripod enables you to take pin-sharp pictures at exposures of longer than the 1/30 second or so which is the longest time generally recommended for a hand-held camera with a standard lens. Long exposures may be necessary (1) in low light; (2) when motion blur is required in relatively slow-moving

Left: even if you have no tripod and cable release you can still take pictures at slow shutter speeds by this method, but it is best if your camera has a self timer (a mechanism for delaying the actual exposure until several seconds after the button is pressed). This method has obvious limitations, but it can be useful in an emergency.

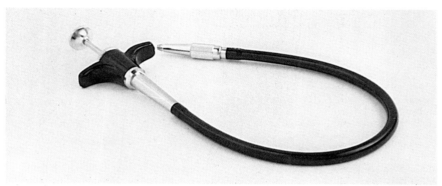

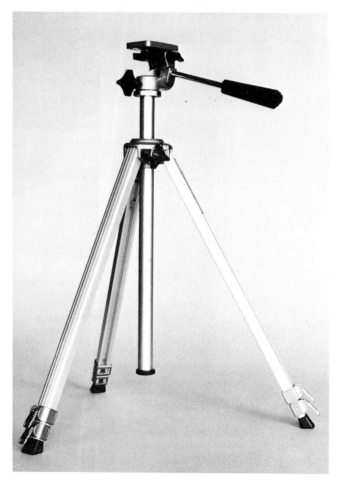

Left: very long lenses are tricky to handle for three main reasons; (1) they are bulkier than standard lenses; (2) they magnify subject movement and hence camera shake, and (3) the relatively small apertures available tend to necessitate fairly slow shutter speeds. For action photography using telephoto lenses (the one illustrated is 400mm) a trigger grip is indispensable.

Opposite page, centre: a cable release. Being flexible this allows the shutter to be released with minimum disturbance to the camera body. It has a locking screw just above the finger grips, so that if the camera has a B setting exposures of minutes or even hours can be made.

Opposite page, bottom: tripods. The one on the left is light and inexpensive, but versatile. The legs extend and can be locked at any height, as can the central column, which can also be reversed for close-up or copying work. The pan and tilt head can be moved in any plane. The tripod on the right is more rugged, although its range of movements is similar. The rubber feet can be extended (as here) for gripping hard surfaces or retracted so that the metal points have a firm hold on soft ones.

Right: a Pentax battery grip, which acts as a power unit for the motor drive and doubles as a steadying handle. This is especially valuable if the camera is being used with a bulk film back (illustrated on page 148).

Below: another kind of steadying handle—this is particularly useful when you need to use flash in an awkward situation, such as in the thick of a jostling crowd. The cable release is built into the handle enabling a much firmer grasp to be maintained, and the hand strap makes it possible to operate the camera with one hand if absolutely necessary. The accessory shoe on the grip is conveniently situated not too near to the lens-to-subject axis, so that a flash unit will not cause the same problems as when it is mounted on top of the camera.

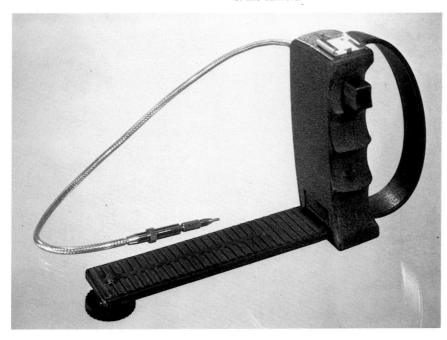

subjects, and (3) for certain special effects such as time-exposures of fireworks, lightning etc. And you will certainly not get the best out of expensive telephoto and macro lenses unless you also have a tripod.

Buy the sturdiest tripod you can afford: a flimsy one is little better than a shaky hand, but a really solid one will make a marked difference to the quality of your pictures. You will also need a *cable release*, preferably one with a locking screw, although for static subjects at exposures not requiring the B setting a self-timer would be adequate.

Apart from tripods there are other camera supports of varying degrees of usefulness; some of those likely to be of interest to the amateur photographer are illustrated here.

Telephoto lenses

A telephoto lens does for the camera what a telescope does for the eye: it magnifies distant objects and creates the illusion that they are closer than they actually are. (A good telephoto lens, fitted to a single-lens reflex camera mounted on a tripod, can be used as an astronomical telescope.)

Technically, a telephoto lens is a lens with a long focal length. The standard lens on a 35mm camera has a focal length of 50mm or thereabouts; anything longer than this and it is called a telephoto. Theoretically there is no limit to focal length, but in practice lenses get more expensive and more difficult to use as they get longer.

It is quite easy to work out what degree of magnification a lens offers relative to the area covered by a standard 50mm lens: simply divide its focal length by 50. Thus a 100mm lens gives × 2 magnification (in other words it fills the frame with exactly half the area of subject); a 200 mm lens will magnify the subject 4 times, so that only a quarter of what you see through a standard lens will appear on the film.

Telephoto lenses and perspective

Taking a photograph of a distant object with a telephoto lens does not give the same result as moving in closer and taking a picture with a standard lens. This is because a telephoto lens simply isolates the subject from its surroundings by reducing the *angle of view* of the camera; if you move closer you alter the spatial relationships between objects relative to the camera, so that a nearby object appears larger than one further away although both may, in fact, be the same size. The only way to achieve a 'telephoto' effect with a standard lens is to enlarge only a small section of the negative, but a degree of graininess and loss of quality will result, and depth of field may be different.

Depth of field

The longer the focal length of a lens, the shallower will depth of field be at any given distance, even if the aperture used is the same. With very long lenses accurate focusing is therefore absolutely critical, particularly at close range.

Below left: a portrait taken with a 135mm lens, demonstrating the shallow depth of field obtained with telephoto lenses used at close range. Foreground leaves are visible only as an ill-defined fuzziness, mostly on the right of the picture, and the background too is distinctly out of focus; the result is that the subject stands out sharply. This is one reason why many portrait photographers favour moderate telephoto lenses (i.e. of around 90-135mm focal length) for much of their work. The effect is even more marked if a wide aperture is used.

It is important to be aware of this property of telephoto lenses, and to make use of it where possible. It is quite common for portrait photographers to use a moderate telephoto – say about 90-135mm on a 35mm camera – because, among other reasons, it is easier to render the background out of focus and concentrate attention on the face of the sitter (and also because the perspective is more flattering to the human face).

Camera shake

Any slight movement of the camera during exposure can spoil a picture if the shutter speed is slow enough to let the movement record on film. Just as a telephoto lens magnifies the subject in proportion with its focal length, so it will magnify any movement of either subject or camera in the same proportion: a tiny trembling of the camera that may be slight enough to go undetected with a 50mm lens will be doubled with a 100mm lens, quadrupled with a 200mm lens, and so on. Therefore

your slowest shutter speed should be roughly halved each time focal length is doubled: if your slowest speed for hand-held photography is 1/30 second with a 50mm lens, it would not be safe to go below 1/60 second with 100mm and 1/125 with a 200mm lens, etc. This problem is further exaggerated by two factors: in the first place telephoto lenses can be rather bulky, so that they are more difficult to hold steady anyway; secondly the maximum aperture (f/stop rather than actual diameter) is reduced with increasing focal length, so it is limited how far you can open up in order to use a faster shutter speed. Trial and error will reveal what shutter speeds you can work with when holding the camera in tricky situations; the most satisfactory solution, however, is to get a good tripod or other support and always use it unless it is quite impossible to do so.

Other problems

No telephoto lens can penetrate distance haze caused by dust in the atmosphere, so it may be possible to

use the longer ones only at fairly close range when the air is not crystal clear. Furthermore there are exposure problems which necessitate through-the-lens light metering. This and the considerations already mentioned lead to one inevitable conclusion: that it is pointless to think about longer lenses except with single-lens reflex viewing.

Opposite page, right: a telephoto lens can be used simply as an aid to composition. Using a 135mm lens the photographer was able to isolate this agreeable snowbound landscape from a confusion of distracting earthworks just out of the picture. If the same area were cropped from a negative taken with a standard lens the grain could become obtrusive, and of course cropping colour transparencies down to less than half of their original size is never fully satisfactory.

This page, left: the use of a 200mm lens has compressed space, piling up the subject and reducing its apparent depth.

Two Super Travenar telephoto lenses. The 300mm lens on the left would magnify to full image size one-sixth of the image area taken in by a standard (50mm) lens, making it a good choice for sports or wildlife photography, where a telescopic effect is required. The 135mm lens on the right, although less impressive to look at, would have many more uses in general photography, and would be a good choice for anyone who is looking for a second or third lens to add to his system.

Wide-angle lenses

In many respects wide-angle lenses can be described as having effects and applications exactly the reverse of those offered by telephoto lenses. They appear to make things more distant than they actually are but, having a wide angle of view, take in more of the scene than a standard lens. Their principal use is in places where the space available to work in is restricted, especially in crowds where the photographer has little room to manoeuvre, and interiors where walls prevent him stepping back to get more into the picture.

The relationship between focal length and coverage (relative to that of a standard lens) is the same as for telephotos: thus a 24mm lens will cover an area just slightly over twice as large, an 18mm lens somewhat over two and a half times as large, and so on. Instead of being magnified, details are of course diminished in size.

Wide-angle lenses and perspective

No matter what lens is being used, the *relative* sizes of objects in front of it will be exactly the same on film as they appear to the eye. Changing lenses makes no difference except to what is included and what is not.

In practice, wide-angle lenses include more of the foreground than those of longer focal lengths, and objects in the foreground *appear* to be disproportionately large. This is an illusion that occurs because the brain compensates for what the eye sees in life, ignoring nearby objects when it is concentrating on more distant ones and vice versa; but it does not compensate for what it sees within the frame of a two-dimensional image, recognizing only a form of distortion.

To obtain wide-angle photographs that look natural it is necessary to make sure that the foreground is not cluttered. This is not to say that your photographs ought always to look natural: on the contrary, it can be great fun to experiment with the apparent distortion characteristic of wide-angle lenses, and to exploit it for its humorous effects.

Depth of field

Just as depth of field is decreased with telephoto lenses, so it is increased with wide-angles. This makes them easier to use in that focusing is not likely to be a problem (although there is no need to get careless about it); it is also one of the reasons why the lenses fitted to fixed-focus cameras are moderate wide-angles.

Extreme wide-angle and fisheye lenses

A fisheye lens is an extreme form of wide-angle—so wide, in fact, that it takes in an angle of up to 180° or sometimes even more. This is so wide that the human eye cannot take it in all at once. Yet this vast area is recorded on the same piece of film.

This photograph of a cornfield by the sea gives an idea of the great impression of depth that can be achieved by using a wide-angle lens. One of 28mm focal length, such as was used here, will include almost double the amount of subject area that a standard 50mm lens would cover.

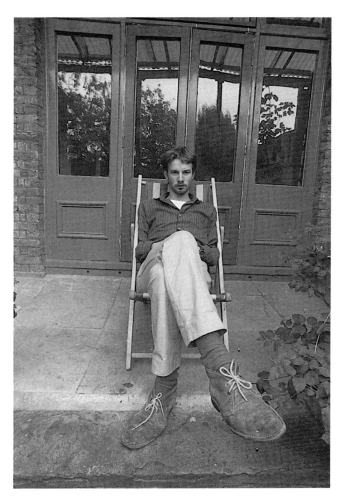

Above: seen through a wide-angle lens objects close to the camera appear to be disproportionately large, becoming more normal-looking as they get further away. The effect is most unnatural with objects of known size—and everyone knows that a person's head would not really fit into his shoe, although this picture suggests it might. Avoid creating this distortion by not having some parts of a subject much closer to the camera than others, unless, of course, you wish to make a deliberately humorous or insulting portrait.

Above right: this picture is 'distorted' in much the same way as the one next to it, but here it is far less evident. This is because we do not instinctively know whether the rocks in the foreground are large boulders or ordinary pebbles; also, over greater distances the eye is accustomed to the effects of perspective, so it does not 'read' the tower and the nearest stones as being the same size. Note also that in all the pictures reproduced on these pages depth of field extends from the front of the picture to the back.

Below: two Super Travenar wide-angle lenses. The one on top has a focal length of 35mm, the one below a focal length of 28mm. The shorter a lens becomes the more difficult it is to handle it convincingly, so if you are buying one for the first time it is probably best to avoid lenses of 24mm or less; go instead for one of around 35mm focal length.

The shortest fisheyes of all give a circular image within the normal rectangular film area, and unless they cross the centre of the image lines appear to be curved, the more so the nearer they are to the edge of the frame.

This looks like a violent distortion, which is what it is when presented on a flat piece of paper. (To be a true record of what the camera 'saw' the image would have to be printed or projected on to the inside of a hemispherical surface such as a pudding bowl, with the viewer's eye at the centre, at equal distance from every part of the image.)

Extreme wide-angles and fisheyes need very large, good quality elements at the front, and good ones are therefore necessarily expensive. The amateur should think carefully before investing in any lens of extreme focal length unless he has definite reasons for believing that he will use it a good deal. The results, although spectacular at first, tend to look monotonous after a while; the chances are that the money could be better spent on other accessories or on a large stock of film.

Other special lenses

Zoom

A zoom lens is one with a continuously variable focal length, so that in
effect it replaces a whole set of lenses
of fixed focal length. Its great advantage is that it enables the photographer to frame his subject precisely
without having either to move
backwards or forwards, or to remove
one lens and fit another.

Zoom lenses are identified by two
figures representing their shortest and
longest focal lengths. They vary
greatly in their range, falling broadly
into the same wide-angle, standard
and telephoto categories as their
fixed counterparts. When focusing
and zooming are both controlled by
a single ring (push/pull to zoom,
rotate to focus) this is known as
one-touch zoom; other types, usually
in the wide-angle to standard range,
have independent zooming and
focusing rings.

Once the focal length has been
selected for any subject the same
consideration should be given to
depth of field, shutter speed and so
on as for a fixed lens of that focal
length.

Zoom lenses are complicated in
design and good ones are inevitably
rather expensive, but their versatility
may make them a worthwhile
investment for single-lens reflex users.

**Above: altering the focal length of
a lens, or 'zooming', as the exposure
is made can create this effect. You
need a fairly slow shutter speed, a
suitable subject and some practice in
the technique of zooming smoothly.**

**Far left: the Sunagor 80-205mm zoom
lens, which also has a macro setting.**

**Left: the Tamron SP 350mm tele macro
—a compact mirror lens with macro
facility. The disc in the front
element is one of the mirrors.**

Mirror

Lenses of extremely long focal length become very bulky. Mirrors, used in place of certain clear glass lens elements, reflect the light entering the front of the lens back and forth in such a way that a long light path can be compressed into a shorter space, combining telephoto performance with light weight and compact design. There are drawbacks, however: the design of mirror lenses is such that the diaphragm cannot be varied in size, so that exposure can be controlled by shutter speed and/or the use of neutral density filters only. Out-of-focus highlights appear as rings rather than discs—an unavoidable effect but one which is not altogether displeasing.

Teleconverters

Supplementary lenses known as teleconverters or telephoto converters can be used to increase the focal length of any lens by a constant factor, usually 2 or 3. Thus a standard 50mm lens fitted with a × 2 teleconverter becomes a 100mm lens, a 135mm becomes a 270mm lens, and so on. Although image quality suffers slightly, the system is relatively cheap and offers a convenient alternative to carrying many bulky lenses around.

Teleconverters can be used with all interchangeable lenses including zooms; thus the range of, say, a 75-150mm zoom is extended from 150mm up to 300mm. Note also that the f/stops given on the converted lens will no longer be correct because of the increase in focal length, so through-the-lens metering should be used.

Above: imaginative use of a macro lens (or, to be exact, a zoom lens with a macro setting, like the one illustrated on the opposite page). The lens was focused on the spider and carefully placed so that the insect was just contained by the disc of the sun. The harsh contrast has inevitably made the spider come out as a silhouette, but this only enhances the menacing quality of the picture.

Below: on Derby day, unable to see the race itself because there were too many people, the photographer turned his zoom lens on the professional lensmen to photograph this amazing array of expensive optics. The photograph on the left was taken at 70mm focal length, that on the right moments later at 150mm. The price of such lenses is now quite reasonable, especially considering that they can replace a number of lenses of fixed focal lengths.

Built-in exposure meters

An exposure meter (also known as a *light meter*) is a device for measuring the amount of light in a given scene, so that the camera controls can be set to yield a correctly exposed photograph every time. The main component is a light-sensitive cell which reacts to light by regulating an electric current produced by batteries. The current activates a needle or a digital display and this, read in conjunction with the film speed, gives the correct exposure value.

Nearly all 35mm single-lens reflexes and rangefinder cameras have a built-in exposure meter of the through-the-lens (TTL) type. This means that it is *only* the light reaching the film that is measured—a system that is generally easy to use and has obvious advantages. Any camera that claims to be automatic or semi-automatic must of course have a built-in metering system, although in the case of some fully automatic models there is no need for the user to be aware of it at all. A camera with a TTL metering system will give perfectly exposed pictures most of the time, but there are situations in which the photographer needs to use his skill to override the meter indication.

Not all TTL systems are identical. The main difference lies in what part of the scene they take the reading from. An *average reading* meter reads the light from all over the image area, so that light and dark areas balance each other out; a *centre weighted* meter reads from a large area but is increasingly sensitive towards the centre of the frame (the somewhat questionable assumption being that this is where the main area of interest will be); and a *spot* meter reads only a small circle marked in the centre of the frame. The spot metering system is the most accurate when properly used, but it does require the photographer to choose carefully which spot he is going to meter, otherwise a more or less arbitrary reading can result.

How to use a TTL meter

Before you use a camera manually with TTL metering, make sure you know which of the above systems is used—the manufacturer's manual should tell you this. Whenever you take a reading think about what is being metered: is it the most important part of the scene, and is it of average brightness? An exposure meter will always attempt to *darken* bright subjects and *lighten* dark ones, so either take your reading from an area of neutral brightness or estimate by how many stops you should alter the metered reading to compensate for the special lighting qualities of the subject.

In any situation where contrast is high it is easy to be misled by a built-in meter. If necessary move close to the subject so as to exclude a contrasting background which may influence the meter, then set the camera manually, overriding the automatic function, before stepping back to take the photograph from the desired position. If your camera is an automatic with no manual override, alter the film speed setting instead.

For example, if you have a 200 ASA film loaded, change the setting to 400 ASA to underexpose by one stop, 800 ASA to underexpose by two stops, or to 100 or 50 ASA to overexpose by one or two stops respectively.

A centre spot meter can be pointed at different parts of the scene, both light and dark in turn, and an average reading worked out. But the real advantage of this system is that it becomes easier to choose between exposing for the highlights and exposing for the shadows. Bear in mind that in the finished photograph the area covered by the central spot will be of medium brightness if the reading is followed, so that if the camera is pointed at a brightly illuminated face against a dark background, for example, the face will record correctly and the background will be very dense; but if the face is off-centre the meter will read the shadows instead and detail will be retained in these while the face becomes overexposed and washed out.

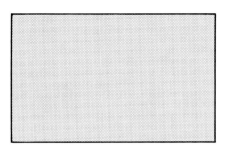 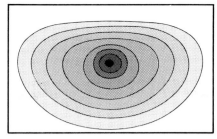 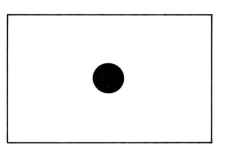

Above: the three common through-the-lens (TTL) exposure metering systems. From left to right: average reading, centre weighted and spot (see text).

The blackberries (opposite page) and the snow scene (right) are examples of subjects that will mislead any TTL metering system. A meter cannot differentiate between a black (or white) subject and dark (or bright) conditions, and it will give readings which, if followed, would result in these two pictures being an identical mid-grey shade. In cases such as these the meter must be ignored or, with automatic cameras, overriden. The blackberries were photographed out of doors and the photographer established the correct reading by pointing the camera away from them; this clearly would not work for the snow picture, so the photographer had to estimate how much he should 'overexpose' by.

Below: two photographs, taken within moments of each other, of exactly the same subject. For the one on the left a meter reading was taken with the camera pointing outside the merry-go-round, with the result that its interior is badly underexposed. For that on the right the reading was taken with the camera pointing down at the floor, so that the merry-go-round has retained plenty of detail, while the sunny background is entirely bleached out.

Hand-held exposure meters

Hand-held exposure meters are rather more trouble to use, but ultimately more accurate than built-in meters. In the majority of cases a built-in meter, used intelligently, is quite adequate for amateur use. Independent metering is mostly useful for owners of adjustable cameras without built-in meters—not common nowadays unless passed down from another generation—and for advanced large-format studio work.

Until recently the most common types have been the selenium cell meter, which produces its own electric current in response to being struck by light, and the cadmium sulphide (CdS) meter, which works by regulating a current produced by batteries. Built-in meters are almost always of the cadmium sulphide type as this has greater sensitivy in low light. The latest generation of light meters has a silicon photo diode as its main component; this is also battery operated but has the additional advantage of being able to adapt instantly from very bright to very dim lighting conditions, which a CdS meter cannot do.

How to use a hand-held meter

There are two ways to use a hand-held meter. It can be held level with the camera and pointing towards the subject: this is known as taking a *reflected light* reading. The drawback here is that subject or background qualities, if they are not typical, can throw the reading seriously out as described for built-in meters on page 145. A more precise reflected light reading can be obtained with a spot meter, which is rather like a single-lens reflex camera without film. The photographer looks through a lens at roughly the same image area as is presented by a standard lens, with a small circle marked in the centre. The meter measures only the light from this spot, so that an accurate measurement can be taken from a single important point, or a series of readings can be taken and an average calculated.

The other way to use a hand-held

meter is to fit it with a diffuser and hold it up to the subject, pointing in the general direction of the light source. This is known as an *incident light* reading, and is extremely accurate as it measures the actual light falling on a scene before the subject qualities have imparted their own variables to it. An incident light reading is obviously not practicable where circumstances may change from one moment to the next and quick reactions are necessary.

Sophisticated exposure meters can

be adapted to take either reflected or incident light readings, and the most up to date models often have a memory function so that a number of readings can be stored and compared.

Below: using a Weston Master exposure meter to take (top) a reflected light reading with the light-sensitive cell pointing towards the subject, and (bottom) an incident light reading with the cell covered by a light-diffusing cap (Invercone), pointing in the direction of the light source. When time and conditions permit, the second method is the most accurate of all the ways of measuring light.

Above: in high-contrast situations the exposure needs to be measured very accurately so that shadow areas do not drop away into solid black and detail is not bleached out in the highlights. If the range of contrast is beyond what the film can record, no amount of metering will help; the photographer must then decide whether to expose for highlights or shadows.

Below: a Zodel meter (front) with a needle exposure value indicator. This works on the same principle as the famous Weston Master meters, shown here with and without the Invercone. The meter at the back is a Pentax digital spot meter—this measures the light reflected from tiny or distant areas with microchip accuracy.

Above: one of the Soligor range of exposure meters. The film speed is set in the window low down on the right of the dial, and the exposure value indicated by the needle is transferred to the dial. It is then converted by the scale into options ranging from shutter speeds of 8 minutes to 1/8000 second and apertures of f/1 to f/45— more than enough for most people.

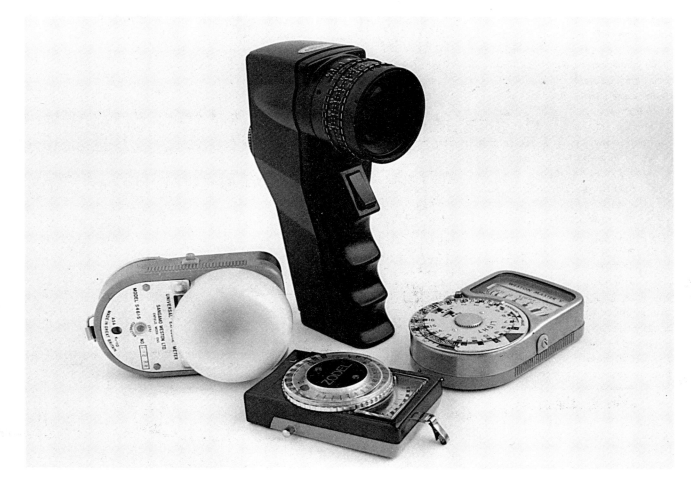

Other accessories — some useful additions to your system

You can take up photography as a hobby even if you possess nothing more than a pocket camera and some film. But many people who start out on this modest scale begin to feel after a while that they could do so much more, if only they owned this or that piece of equipment. If you have a pocket camera or other simple non-adjustable model, the first step will be to upgrade to a more versatile system—probably to a single-lens reflex with its interchangeable lens facility. This need not be an expensive transition, particularly if your dealer will accept your old equipment in part exchange; otherwise it can always be kept as a back-up camera—perhaps for experimenting with black and white work, or to lend to the children for their holidays.

The accessories which by general agreement do most to widen the photographer's horizons—filters, tripods, flash and so on—are examined more fully elsewhere in this book. Some of the items described here are less universally useful, but may be of interest to those who become absorbed in any particular branch of photography, or to those who have heard a bit about them and are curious to know more.

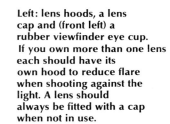

Left: lens hoods, a lens cap and (front left) a rubber viewfinder eye cup. If you own more than one lens each should have its own hood to reduce flare when shooting against the light. A lens should always be fitted with a cap when not in use.

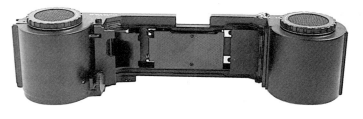

Above: the Pentax bulk film back, designed to hold 250 exposures of 35mm film.

Left: the motor winder, part of the same Pentax 35mm system. The unit is battery powered and winds the film on automatically after each exposure, enabling a rapid but controlled sequence of shots to be taken.

The motor drive differs from the winder in that as long as the release button is kept depressed the camera will continue to shoot automatically at a rate of up to 5 frames per second. The user can choose the number of frames/second within the limitations imposed by the duration of each exposure. The motor drive, if kept going at maximum speed, would empty the bulk film back shown above in 50 seconds.

Below: a single-lens reflex fitted with motor drive was used to take this sequence of shots showing a backhand tennis stroke. Motor drives are much used by sports and action photographers, either to make sure of getting at least one good shot or in order to analyze a sportsman's technique. They are also of value to anyone who wishes to study the mechanics of movement.

But first a word of caution: do not be tempted to buy expensive accessories unless you are fairly certain that you will get your money's worth of use out of them. This applies to *all* accessories – to filter systems, long lenses, powerful flash units and anything else – not just to the items shown here. Equipment often looks extremely impressive, and it is easy to imagine that it will be as useful as it is glamorous; but how often do you actually need a lens of 1000mm focal length – just once to try it out, or fairly frequently? And when you have seen your first set of pictures with starburst effects, will you ever want to create them again?

Complicated equipment does not guarantee success. It might be better to spend money on an abundant supply of film, which will give you the freedom to experiment and become successful with the equipment you already own. So the moral is, think before you buy.

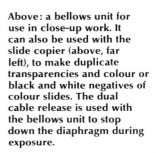

Above, centre: a long cable release which is operated by an air bulb, mostly used for group and self-portraits, animal photographs, etc.

Below: the Pentax data back. This can be fitted instead of the normal camera back to record details of date and exposure direct on to the film. It is useful for the busy photographer who needs to keep accurate and detailed records.

Above: a bellows unit for use in close-up work. It can also be used with the slide copier (above, far left), to make duplicate transparencies and colour or black and white negatives of colour slides. The dual cable release is used with the bellows unit to stop down the diaphragm during exposure.

Above: extension tubes, which can be used singly or together to make close focusing possible within certain limits. They are considerably cheaper than the bellows unit above, but not so versatile.

Right: Pentax stereo SLR equipment. When fitted in place of the standard lens this gives two nearly identical half-frame images which, when viewed through the stereo viewer, create a three-dimensional effect.

Equipment care and maintenance

Good cameras are made to endure rigorous assignments and be reliable in far-flung corners of the world where there is no repair shop just round the corner, and for that reason they have to be very rugged indeed. Any well-known make should be able to withstand many years of amateur use without problems. All the same, negligence can easily shorten the working life of your equipment. Looking after it is largely a matter of common sense.

Cleaning

Never use anything other than a blower brush to clean inside a camera. Although strong the mechanism is highly intricate and performance will be impaired if dirt and grit accumulate inside, or if sticks or wires are poked into it. A light dusting with the blower brush in between films should be enough to keep things in working order and prevent the film getting scratched as it is wound on: hold the part being cleaned upside-down so that particles of dust and grit fall out rather than disappear into the mechanism when dislodged by the brush.

Always shut the camera back and put a cap on the front, whether or not a lens is left in place, when you are not changing the film or taking a photograph.

Above: a blower brush is a simple but effective item of cleaning equipment. Dust the interior of your camera with one of these in between films.

Left: a lens cleaning outfit such as the Minette kit shown here will often come in useful.

Opposite page, top: the Quest range of camera bags includes everything from small ones carrying a 110 pocket camera to capacious holdalls designed to take film and accessories as well as cameras and lenses.

Opposite page, bottom: some of the worst enemies of photographic equipment are the very substances it is most likely to come into contact with—sand, salt spray and the heat of the summer sun. Avoid having to leave a camera exposed to the elements.

Lens cleaning tissues can be used to clean dusty optics, but first brush out loose dust with the blower brush, then rub *gently* and not vigorously with the tissues: the glass used for lenses is softer than ordinary glass and is easily scratched.

Storage

It would be gratifying to think that photographic equipment need never be stored for long periods; but if you do need to put your camera and any spare lenses and accessories away for a while the following precautions are recommended.

Put them in a dustproof place that is not subject to extremes of temperature and humidity; remove any batteries; pack a small bag of silica gel with each item; make sure that any openings are closed, i.e. caps on lenses, camera back shut, battery compartments shut, and so on. If there is a half-finished film in the camera, finish it and send it away for processing.

Repairs

If something does go wrong with your camera take it to a repair shop—do not even begin to think about trying to do it yourself. Ask them for an estimate of the cost before letting them start work.

If you think your camera or lenses need oiling you are mistaken. The only lubricant that should be considered is powdered graphite—and that only sparingly and in accordance with the equipment maker's instructions.

Care while in use

Although many cameras can tolerate a considerable amount of ill-treatment in the field there is no need to subject them to it gratuitously.

Seaside holidays can be particularly hard on cameras, with the combined hazards of sand, sea and salt spray, sun, and probing little fingers. Fit a skylight or UV filter over the lens if you can: either of these will act as a permanent lens protector which need not be removed for picture taking. The same applies in inclement weather and any place where there is a lot of dust in the atmosphere. Try not to leave photographic equipment (including film) lying in direct sun, and certainly not on the beach.

Glossary

A

Angle of view the widest angle at which light rays entering a lens will still give a full image on the film plane.

Aperture the opening in a lens which controls the amount of light passing through the lens; usually variable in diameter.

ASA rating (American Standards Association) indicates the speed, or sensitivity to light, of film. The higher the ASA number, the faster the film. Film speed doubles as its ASA rating doubles; 400 ASA film, for example, is twice as fast as 200 ASA film.

Automatic exposure control automatic adjustment of either lens aperture or shutter speed or both to suit the lighting conditions.

B

Backlighting lighting from behind the subject.

Bellows lightproof folding tube which can be fitted between the lens and the camera body for close-up photography.

Blower brush soft brush and air bulb combined, useful for cleaning delicate equipment.

Bounced flash flash illuminating a subject indirectly by reflection off a ceiling or a wall.

Bracketing taking a series of pictures instead of a single one, varying only in the exposure.

B setting setting at which the shutter will remain open as long as the shutter release remains depressed.

C

Cable release flexible cable which can be fixed into the shutter release button, helping reduce camera shake when the camera is mounted on a tripod.

Cadmium sulphide meter exposure meter which works by regulating an electric current produced by batteries.

Camera shake in hand-held photography, the slight but unavoidable movement of the hands which results in a greater or lesser degree of blurring at shutter speeds of less than 1/30 second or thereabouts.

Colour temperature measurement of the colour quality of light.

Contact prints prints made the same size as the negatives with the printing paper in direct contact with the negatives.

Converging verticals the effect of perspective by which parallel lines appear to approach each other with increasing distance from the eye; this looks normal in the horizontal plane (e.g. railway tracks) but 'distorted' in the vertical plane (e.g. the walls of buildings).

Cropping trimming a photograph to alter or improve the composition, remove distracting detail etc.

D

Depth of field distance between the nearest and furthest point from the camera within which the subject is in focus.

Differential focusing setting the lens aperture for minimum depth of field, to limit focus to a particular subject against a background and/or foreground that is out of focus.

DIN rating (Deutsche Industrie Normen) film speed scale sometimes preferred to the ASA rating. For a fuller comparison see pages 42–43.

E

Electronic flash flash produced when an electric current stored in a capacitor is discharged into a gas-filled tube.

Electronic shutter shutter where the period between opening and closing is regulated automatically.

Enlarger type of projector used to focus a negative image on to printing paper to produce prints of different sizes by increasing or decreasing the distance between the negative and the paper.

Enprint standard sized print, about 12 × 9cm–slightly smaller than an ordinary postcard.

Exposure the volume of light that reaches the film (controlled by the lens aperture) multiplied by the length of time (controlled by shutter speed).

Exposure latitude the margin of error within which over or underexposed negatives or prints are still acceptable.

Exposure meter instrument that measures the amount of light being reflected by a subject.

Extension tube tube that fits between lens and camera body to extend the range of focusing for close-up photography in a series of fixed steps.

F

f/stops sequence of numbers engraved on the lens barrel equivalent to the focal length divided by diameter of the aperture.

Filter disc or square which modifies light passing through it. Colour filters absorb certain wavelengths of light; this has the effect of causing colours complementary to that of the filter to darken and similar colours to lighten.

Fisheye lens extreme wide-angle lens.

Flare light scattered by reflections within the lens. May appear as a series of blobs each in the shape of the aperture.

Focal length the distance between the back of the lens and the focal plane when the lens is focused on infinity.

Focal plane the plane at right angles to the lens axis on which a sharp image is formed by the lens and at which the film is situated during exposure.

Focus the point at which light rays from the lens converge to give a clear and sharp image of the subject.

G

Glossy paper printing paper with a smooth, shiny surface.

Grain tiny clumps of black silver formed in an emulsion after exposure and development.

Guide number number used to determine the aperture required with any given unit-to-subject distance when flash is used.

H

Highlights lightest parts of the image; the opposite of shadows.

Hot shoe accessory shoe on top of a camera body with guide rails to hold a flash unit. It makes an electrical connection between flash unit and shutter mechanism, so that the flash is fired at the right moment.

I

Infinity camera-to-subject distance beyond which focusing differences are so slight as to be non-existant for practical purposes.

Instamatic camera basic camera which takes cartridges of film, and so can be loaded instantly.

Instant photography system which produces a processed print immediately after exposure direct from the camera.

L

Latent image the invisible image formed on the emulsion when a photograph is taken.

M

Macro lens lens especially designed for extreme close-up photography.

Modelling surface undulations or irregularities emphasized by skilful use of light and shade.

Monochrome technical term for black and white (literally meaning 'of a single colour').

Motor drive battery-operated motor which automatically advances the film and fires the shutter continuously, taking a rapid sequence of exposures at a (sometimes) variable rate of frames per second.

Motor winder battery-operated motor which automatically advances the film when an exposure has been made (but does not fire the shutter).

N

Negative photographic image in which subject highlights are dark and shadows light; used in an enlarger to make a positive image on printing paper.

P

Panning the technique of swinging the camera to follow a moving subject so that the subject stands out sharply against a blurred, streaked background.

Parallax the difference between the area seen through the viewfinder and that covered by the picture-taking lens, negligible at normal distances becoming increasingly marked in close-up work (not applicable with single-lens reflex viewing systems).

Perspective the impression of depth and distance created by the relative size of objects at different positions and by the apparent convergence of parallel lines.

Plate camera camera originally designed for use with glass plates instead of flexible film.

Plates large-format light-sensitive materials with the emulsion coated on glass (now rarely used).

Polarizing filter colourless filter that absorbs polarized light; used to cut out glare from reflected light.

Prefocusing focusing not on the subject but on a point through which the subject is expected to pass, and not taking the photograph until the precise moment when it does so.

Print an enlarged image produced on paper coated with a light-sensitive emulsion; made from a negative in an enlarger.

Projector piece of equipment used to display enlarged images, preferably on to a screen.

Push-processing see Uprating.

R

Rangefinder a focusing system that determines the distance from camera to subject.

Reciprocity the relationship between lens aperture and shutter speed, which is so designed that the step between adjacent settings on either scale always increases or decreases the exposure by the same factor.

Red eye effect producing red eyes in colour portraits taken by flash. The retina, which is red, reflects flash light into the camera lens if the unit is too close to the camera-lens axis.

Retouching hand treating of negatives or prints to remove spots and blemishes.

Selenium cell meter exposure meter which works by producing an electric current when struck by light; now largely superseded by the cadmium sulphide meter which has a faster reaction time when subjected to extremes of lighting levels.

S

Self-timer a mechanism built into many cameras which delays the release of the shutter for several seconds after the button is pressed.

Single-lens reflex (SLR) camera which allows the user to see in the viewfiinder the exact image formed on the film by means of a mirror behind the lens. The mirror is raised when the shutter is open.

Slave unit relay mechanism which fires other flash units simultaneously with the unit connected to the camera.

Slide *see* Transparency.

Soft focus romantic effect achieved by the use of a soft focus filter or other attachment placed either on the camera or enlarger lens.

Split-image focusing focusing system in which a small part of the image is split and remains out of alignment until the lens is correctly focused.

Standard lens camera lens which will give an angle of view and a scale that approximates to human vision (usually 50mm in single lens reflex cameras).

Stereoscopic photography system of producing three-dimensional images by dividing the picture into two nearly identical halves and displaying them simultaneously by means of a special viewer or projector.

T

Teleconverter or **telephoto converter** supplementary lens which can be used to increase the focal length of any lens with which it is combined.

Telephoto lens lens with a narrow angle of view, which effectively magnifies distant objects.

Through-the-lens (TTL) metering a system of measuring only the light that actually passes through the lens, leading to a very accurate exposure.

Time exposure a long exposure made by opening and closing the shutter manually with the shutter release at the B setting.

Transparency positive image, usually in colour, made using reversal film.

Tripod three-legged adjustable camera stand.

Tungsten lighting artificial lighting such as that given by ordinary domestic lamp bulbs.

U

Uprating overdeveloping a film to compensate for (deliberate) underexposure; effectively increases film speed.

W

Wide-angle lens lens with a short focal length and hence wide angle of view.

Z

Zoom lens lens with a continuously variable focal length, and which can therefore replace a number of lenses of fixed focal lengths.

Acknowledgements

Catherine Blackie contents page (2), 16t, 20, 21t, 26tl, 69tl, 75b, 82b, 83t, 84b, 93br, 96tl, 105tl, 108t, 110br, 111tl, 113bl, 116lr, 117t, 117br, 114tr; **Mark Bleiweiss** 80t; **Martin Brown** 49c; **Colour Library International** 119t; **Peter Crump** endpapers, contents page (1), 15, 32ct, 32cb, 32b, 34t, 34ct, 34cb, 40b, 41t, 54l, 57tl, 62b, 65tr, 65tl, 70r, 73tr, 76t, 77tl, 77cl, 85tr, 90t, 90b, 91tr, 91tl, 93bl, 94t, 96br, 98r, 99t, 101tr, 105tr, 108br, 109b, 110t, 112r, 112l, 115c, 121b, 123br, 126br, 126bl, 127b, 128br, 133b, 138r, 138l, 141l, 142t, 145t; **Dennis Dracup** 109c; **Geoff du Feu** 17t, 24t, 31r, 34b, 42t, 52r, 52c, 52l, 61tr, 61tl, 61b, 66t, 76b, 77tr, 77cr, 77b, 78b, 81tr, 85tl, 89tr, 94b, 99c, 101tl, 111b, 128bl, 143t, 143br, 143bl; **Karel Feuerstein** 83c, 113br; **Brian Folkard** 83b; **Charles Fowkes** back jacket tl, 86b, 103tl; **Roger Fuller** 147tl; **David Halford** 67t, 78t, 79c, 95tl, 95c, 102l; **Hamlyn Group Picture Library** 25tl, 25cl, 25b, 28, 38, 39, 48b, 49b, 53t, 53c, 54r, 59c, 64, 80b, 81tl, 81b, 89b, 107t, 110bl, 111tr, 114tr, 124t, 125tr, 148–9b; **Hamlyn Group Picture Library – Peter Loughran** 93t, 95b, 97t, 119b; **Michael Herridge** 43b, 62tr, 63b, 85br, 92l; **Leigh Jones** front jacket ct, 13t, 26b, 50t, 63t, 68b, 79t, 82t, 96tr, 103tr, 105br, 106b, 123bl; **Lim Mei-Lan** 86t; **Peter Loughran** 88t, 100t, 120b; **Karen MacDonald** 30, 71t, 74b, 87b, 128t; **Peter MacDonald** back jacket tr, 15r, 18t, 18b, 19b, 26tr, 29, 31l, 32t, 33t, 36t, 36b, 37, 40tr, 40tl, 41b, 42b, 45tl, 46br, 47tl, 48t, 51t, 51b, 55l, 56t, 56b, 57bl, 58, 59bl, 60l, 69t, 71c, 71b, 72t, 73tl, 85tl, 88b, 91b, 92r, 93cr, 95tr, 107br, 107bl, 117bl, 120t, 121tr, 126t, 129, 131, 133t, 133br, 135bl, 139l, 144, 145br, 145bl, 151b; **Michael Mackenzie** 69b, 75tr, 89tl, 91ct, 104b, 106t, 122t, 122b, 124b, 125b; **Luiz Marigo** 144b; **Peter Marshall** 24b, 33b, 35, 43t, 44t, 45tr, 45b, 46t, 46bl, 53br, 57tr, 57br, 63c, 68t, 70l, 72b, 73b, 74t, 75tl, 75c, 87tr, 87tl, 103br, 103bl, 104t, 118b, 135t, 140; **David Morgan** 113t; **Ian Muggeridge** front jacket tr & tl, 22b, 47tr, 55r, 59br, 62tl, 66b, 79b, 84t, 87c, 91c, 96bl, 97b, 98l, 99b, 102r, 108bl, 115t, 115b, 121tl, 123t, 125tl, 127t; **R. K. Pilsbury F.R.P.S.** 100b, 101b; **Martin Reeves** back jacket b; **Royal Shakespeare Company** 118t; **Justin Shepherd** 59t; **Judy Todd** title page, 93cl, 105cb, 105bl.

Artwork on pages 12–13, 14, 20, 22, 31, 32, 34, 37, 51 supplied by Hayward Art Group.

We should also like to thank Pentax U.K. Ltd. for the loan of equipment shown on pages 137, 147, 148, 149.

Key to the photographs used in this book

Many of the photographs reproduced in this book to illustrate specific subjects or techniques may be good examples of other aspects of photography; for example, there is a picture on page 84 in the 'Sun and sunsets' section which clearly demonstrates some of the effects characteristic of telephoto lenses. The following keys are designed to enable interested readers to track down a variety of pictures illustrating particular subjects or the use of specific techniques or equipment. They are for general guidance only and are not intended to be comprehensive.

t=top   c=centre   b=bottom   l=left   r=right

Subject key

Abstract and semi-abstract subjects 57tr; 71tr; 108br
Aeroplanes 26b; 79t; 122b
Animals 31tl; 36b; 40b; 61tl, c; 62b; 69tr; 94b; 142t
Architecture and buildings 29; 46c, br; 65tr; 70bl; 89b; 91tc; 103tr; 147tl
Flowers and plants 36t; 42c; 61tr; 91b
Frost 15br; 44t; 91tl
Mist 8–9; 47tr
Motor racing 34t, ct, cb; 63t; 123bl, br
Night 57tl; 80c; 100; 101
Rain 26cl
Reflections 8–9; 20t; 94t; 104b; 105tr
Sky Endpapers; 64t, c, b; 65tr; 71c; 85tl, tr
Snow Title page; 10–11; 17t; 33b; 56b; 90c; 93cl; 128c; 138r; 145c
Stained glass 72t; 108bl
Street lights 80c; 89tl
Trees 10–11; 19b; 42b; 55tl; 87tl, tr; 94t
Water 8–9; 24t; 34b; 35; 66b; 82b; 85br; 104b; 105tr

Technique key

Artificial background 98l; 126t, br
Backlighting 16c; 36t; 44t; 47tl; 59c; 113br

Camera angle, unusual 75b; 102br; 115c
Camera shake 63c
Close-ups 15br; 18c; 31tr; 98l, r
Colour, subdued 86b; 88t; 101tl
Contrast, high 43b; 47tl; 118b; 139l; 147tl
    low 46br
Cropping 56c, b; 69tl, c
Depth of field, maximum 17t; 41t, b; 45b; 72b; 138l
    minimum 18c; 77cl; 91b; 120c; 124c
Differential focus 40cr, b; 98r
Exposure meter, overriding 33b; 36t, b; 47tl; 79t; 82t, b; 87b; 106c; 107t
Flash, direct 113t
    fill-in 59c
'Freezing' action 111b
Lighting, high key 20t; 56b
    low key 48t
    poor 33t; 48t; 107bl; 108br
Motion-blur effects 34; 35; 54bl; 89tl; 92br; 93bl; 99c; 151b
Panning 78b; 120c, b; 121tr
Prefocusing 120c
Sequences 77r; 81b; 148–149b
Silhouettes Endpapers; 62cl; 76t; 85tl; 143t
Time exposures 88t, b; 89tr, b; 100c, b; 101b

Equipment and materials key

Cable release 77cl
Film, fast (grainy) 43t, b
    for tungsten lighting 118t; 126t
Filter, starburst 24t; 66t; 85tl
Lights, artificial 49t
Reflector (white card) 59c; 111tr
Telephoto lenses 76b; 79c; 84c; 96cl; 122t; 123t; 124c; 125b
Tripod 77cl; 100c, b; 101b
Wide-angle lenses 41t; 94t; 115b; 126br

Index